Clo Storytellers, Disciples

Spirituality and Creativity for Today's Church

Olive M. Fleming Drane

Augsburg Books
MINNEAPOLIS

To my soul mate, John

The author acknowledges financial assistance
toward the writing of this book
from The Drummond Trust,
3 Pitt Terrace, Stirling, Scotland

CLOWNS, STORYTELLERS, DISCIPLES
Spirituality and Creativity for Today's Church

Large-quantity purchases or custom editions of this book are available at a discount from the publisher. For more information, contact the sales department at Augsburg Fortress, Publishers, 1-800-328-4648, or write to: Sales Director, Augsburg Fortress, Publishers, P.O. Box 1209, Minneapolis, MN 55440-1209.

Unless otherwise stated, scripture passages are from the Holy Bible, New International Version, copyright © 1973, 1978, 1984 International Bible Society. Used by permission of Zondervan Publishing House. All rights reserved.

ISBN 0-8066-4949-6

Cover design and cover art by Ann Rezny
Book design by Michelle L. N. Cook

The paper used in this publication meets the minimum requirements of American National Standard for Information Sciences—Permanence of Paper for Printed Library Materials, ANSI Z329.48-1984.

Manufactured in the U.S.A.

08   07   06   05   04   1   2   3   4   5   6   7   8   9   10

Contents

Foreword iv
Introduction v

Part 1: My Stories, God's Story, Your Story
1. A Clown Comes to Birth 2
2. I've Been There Too, Valentine 20
3. Now There Are Two 32
4. A Clown in the Church 41
5. Expanding My Horizons 68
6. Jamaica: Learning from the Poor 78
7. More Teaching and Learning 93

Part 2: The Meaning of It All
8. Spiritual Reflections 104
9. Theological Reflections 123

Part 3: Putting It into Practice
10. Getting from Here to There 142
11. Start with Something Simple 152
12. Bring On the Clowns 167

Conclusion 182
Appendix 1: Creative Bible Study 189
Appendix 2: Some Original Clown Sketches 194
Appendix 3: Destination Bethlehem 203
Other Books on the Arts in Ministry 211
Notes 213

Foreword

The founder of our faith was one of the greatest storytellers of all time. Christian disciples have, since the earliest days, passed their faith on through the stories Jesus told and through the stories that were told about him.

Many modern writers, however, testify to the loss of the storytelling ability in the West. Go to Africa or to the Middle East and people still tell stories in a way that we seem to have forgotten.

I hope that, by bringing the world of clowning to the Christian faith, *Clowns, Storytellers, Disciples* will open the way for Western disciples of Christ to become storytellers again and find fresh insight and inspiration from the master storyteller himself.

—The Rt. Rev. Tom Butler,
Bishop of Southwark

Introduction

Clowns, Storytellers, Disciples **has been a long time in the**
making. Since it is an account of my personal journey through
the ups and downs of life, by definition it could only ever have
been written with the benefit of hindsight, and with some reflective space between where I am today and where I started from.
It is, in many ways, an intensely personal book, based on my own
search for personal wholeness and spiritual meaning. But
throughout, I have attempted to combine story with reflection in
such a way that I hope it will also provide a foundational
resource for those who might be interested in exploring the arts
and spirituality more deeply, in particular in relation to providing an undergirding theology for clown ministry.

Even after being involved in this ministry for several years, it
still seems astonishing to me that the medium of something
apparently as bizarre as clowning could have provided such powerful therapy for my own deepest hurts, and that it clearly speaks
to others in the same profound way. It is only because of its uni-
versal appeal that I eventually was persuaded to share all this with
a wider audience. Time and time again, as I have told Valentine's
story all around the world and to many different kinds of people,
the response has been the same: "If only you could write this story
down . . . I wish I could give it to my daughter/son/
friend/cousin/neighbor/colleague . . . They have had a real tragedy
in their lives . . . I don't know what to say, but if they could hear
your story then this might just help them." More than once I have
asked myself if the story still needs to be told. But like the biblical

prophets, whenever I have tried to leave it behind I have found it impossible to do so. And so God and I have an understanding. If telling the story stops touching people's lives, I will know that it's time to quit. But while there are those who are saying, "Yes I need to hear this," the story will go on. I suppose that in the first place, I decided to write this book out of a sense of responsibility to help and encourage all those who, over the years, have responded to the story's challenge. Of course, our stories are never static. My own journey of faith continues, and there will always be new growth to look forward to, as well as fresh opportunities and possibilities in sharing the love of God with others.

You will notice that throughout this process, my life has become increasingly enmeshed with others. In many of the stories I include here, other people were involved and often played a key role. Effective spirituality is not explored from a place of superiority, as if I—or anyone else—had all the answers. Nor, for that matter, does personal growth come from imagining that we are worthless, with nothing to contribute. On the contrary, I have discovered that we learn the most when we are alongside others, sharing our own hopes and fears, receiving and giving support. Though the details may be different, I have confidence in sharing my story because I know that many others will find their own stories mirrored here, in a way that will make it possible for them to engage with the experiences, and then journey with me in search of some answers.

Of course, the book's topic is a bit wider than just clowning. As the title suggests, storytelling also features in it, along with dance, mask making and other techniques in the arts that I have used in the course of my own spiritual exploration. What I found, and what I think many readers will discover, is that here is a whole treasure trove of distinctively different ways of articulating and understanding faith—different, that is, from the somewhat book-centered culture in which the Church has most often felt at home. Clowning is just one aspect of this, and I have included other things as a way of encouraging those who may not find themselves drawn to clowning as such, but are searching for some new ways forward in our postmodern culture.

Of course, many people who hear the Valentine story immediately see the possibilities of communicating their faith using clowning and want to get started right away. I have therefore tried to include some pointers that will help such enthusiasts to avoid the major pitfalls. I have to say, though, that there really are no shortcuts. Putting on makeup and a costume will not make you a clown. It may not necessarily make the job of sharing faith any easier. But I can guarantee that, if you take it seriously, in the process you will discover a lot more of yourself, and that alone will enrich your life. You will also discover quite early on that for any art form to become a useful tool of spiritual exploration, you will not have all the necessary resources within yourself.

Some readers will no doubt be wondering what clowns can possibly have to do with serious spirituality anyway, especially if your only experience of clowns up to this point has been a visit to a circus. I remember taking part in an event with Ricki Fulton, a well-known Scottish comedian, and he asked me (in all seriousness, not as a joke), "Clowns in church? I've never heard of such a thing!" He is not the only one to have made that sort of comment, and in response I am often tempted to ask, only slightly tongue-in-cheek, "And which church do you go to, not to have met any clowns?" But there is a distinctive quality about being a Christian clown, whether in the circus or the church. The supreme model for the Christian clown is Jesus, and our clowning must bear witness to him. Putting it in the simplest terms, the Christian clown will step in and receive the custard pie in her own face, rather than throw the custard pie at someone else. Actually, clowns have been part of church life for centuries. Even the apostle Paul invited his readers to become "fools" (1 Corinthians 1:20-29), and we find mention of clowns in the technical sense operating in the earliest centuries of the Church, while by the Middle Ages the Holy Fool had a recognizable part to play in the liturgy. We will meet some of these characters in the pages that follow.

We will all recognize different types of clowns from the circus. The Pierrot is the white-faced clown who is always immaculately dressed, with finely defined makeup. In the circus, this clown is often the leader and frequently gets quite cross with the Auguste clowns, who are the ones with big sloppy clothes, often wearing braces attached to trousers which they "lose." They sport white faces with large amounts of paint to elaborate their eyes and mouths, and often have a large false nose. These clowns usually do a lot of very clever acrobatics while making them look like a "mere trip." They are frequently the butt of everyone's jokes, but they are irrepressible and rise up time and time again over every obstacle. The third major category is the down-at-heel tramp whom everyone feels sorry for. Charlie Chaplin is probably the most famous example of this type, and best remembered for his silent films. Just one of the decisions that an aspiring clown has to make is whether they are going to be a speaking or a silent clown.

In recent years the European clown has developed a convention of using much less makeup, often having minimum colors on flesh tone. The clothes have also become less ostentatious. One of the things that I find most interesting about this particular art form is that so far, wherever I have travelled in the world I have found a traditional clown character in every culture. Clowning, even more than some of the other things described in this book, offers an immediate language that transcends cultures, and if the clown is also a mime, that includes the hurdles of the spoken language.

Finally, let me say a word here about how I have set this book out. The various episodes that I describe are told in roughly chronological order, especially in part 1, though they are interspersed with reflections. In part 2, I have returned to some particular aspects of the story in order to highlight some new feature that wouldn't necessarily have been relevant earlier on, before moving on in part 3 to provide some practical guidance for those who might wish to begin experimenting in the context of church life. In organizing things this way, I have been consciously informed by the kind of methodologies now being explored by theologians all over the world, beginning with praxis (my story, my experience of life and of God), followed by reflection on that, asking such questions as "How does this relate to the Bible stories, to Christian tradition, to our wider human experience?" and then returning to ask how our praxis might be reshaped and expressed as we move forward to articulate an appropriate spirituality and theology for today's world, that will be both faithful to our roots while also having a relevance for discipleship in the 21st century.[1] In that sense, this is not therefore a story about the past, but a never-ending story that, it seems to me, has within it the power to take us forward into God's surprising future. But to grasp something of that, you will need to journey with me through the next few chapters and see for yourself.

PART 1

My Stories,
God's Story,
Your Story

Chapter 1

A Clown Comes to Birth

Though I didn't know it at the time, I was part of one of the first groups of generational consumers identified by late 20th-century marketing consultants. I was—and am—a baby boomer, born in the aftermath of World War II, and raised in a Britain that was suffering the consequences of the pain experienced by at least three generations immediately before me. I inherited the hardships of war and yet by the time I was a teenager in the 1960s, along with my contemporaries I was inspired with the possibilities of a new world that was about to be born, and which I would help to create. All my peers took it for granted that life could only get better, and I myself was an optimist, seeing the possibilities more clearly than the pitfalls.

Childhood Traumas

My life up to that point had hardly predisposed me to sharing in this buoyant outlook. When I was born in Glasgow, there was no way my family could have escaped the consequences of the economic deprivation and shortages of goods faced by the community of which we were a part, living in the streets around the busy shipyards of the River Clyde. I remember being told how, only the week before my parents moved into their third-story flat, all the windows in the neighborhood had been blown out by a bomb blast. The flat itself had just one bedroom, no bathroom, and a toilet squeezed into a narrow space that also contained a coal bunker. As a small child, I remember being reminded of the hardship everyone had suffered, as I was told that but a few years before, one egg per week per person would have been a generous allowance—no doubt to help me get things into perspective as food and other supplies began to become more plentiful.

My parents were committed Christians who, for much of their life up to that point, had worked among the people on the dockside, based in a mission hall that provided working families with not only a place to worship, but also a safe haven in which they might discover that they themselves could be people of value, to God and to other people. I still have vivid memories of the stories I heard about homes that my parents regularly visited, and the poverty that was commonplace in that area. My father initially worked as a "gentlemen's outfitter" in the city, but when I was just five years old he came home one day and announced that he was giving up that paid employment in order to work full-time in the deprived community and further the work of the mission.

The fact that my parents had no financial backing for this move, but still believed it was God's call to them and that therefore God would provide whatever they needed, is itself an eloquent testimony to the extent of their commitment.

It was not all good news for me as a young child, however, and when I was only eight years old things took a decidedly unpleasant turn from my perspective. My father had gone to England on a couple of occasions to help another friend from Glasgow run a beach mission at the seaside, and as a result of seeing the possibility of broadening horizons for their ministry, the decision was made somewhere along the line that, in order for my parents more adequately to fulfill their calling, my mother would go to Canada to spend time with two women from what was then called 'the Children's Bible Mission." These two women had previously visited Scotland, and my mother had been inspired by their reports of what they were doing on the other side of the Atlantic and wanted to learn whatever she could from them.

Looking back to what I now know of the social circumstances in Britain at that time, it was probably quite an adventurous thing for a woman from a working-class background to go to what must have seemed like the other side of the world, unaccompanied by her husband. The only thing I remember about it was that, to my young eyes, these two Canadian women seemed much larger than anyone else I knew, and had a strong smell of perfume—something that I suppose was in short supply in Scotland right then. Images from childhood obviously make a big impact, for it took me a long time to reassess my image of Canadians!

At the same time as my mother was to go off to Canada, my father moved on to a different style of ministry, which involved him travelling from city to city, leading mission events for children. Though I picked up bits and pieces of what was going on, this was still a time when children were very much seen and not heard, and I was not included in the deliberations until the final decision about my own future had been taken. My mother had always said that I was a "daddy's girl" and so it was easy for her to decide that I should not go to Canada, because I would arguably miss my father more than her. It was determined that I would stay behind, but of course my father—being a man of his generation, and also because of the itinerant nature of his work—would not be able to look after me either. So where would I stay? I had very many relatives living in the same or nearby communities in and around Glasgow, but they were not seriously considered as possible guardians because none of them was perceived to have the right sort of religious beliefs. Over and above everything else, whoever I might stay with would have to measure up to a rigorous standard of right doctrine. Eventually I was sent to stay with a family whom I had encountered before, but only briefly. They lived in the town where my father had been working in seaside missions, and I met them for the first time in the summer of 1954 and was then taken to live with them permanently in September 1955.

It was as if someone had flipped a switch: one life was closed down, and another opened the next day. I was moved overnight from a large Scottish urban environment to a small industrial town in northeast England. I changed schools, family, friends—everything—in an instant. I am sure the family with whom I was left genuinely tried their best to make me feel welcome, but my abiding memory is of escaping from the dining table, swallowing hard so as not to cry, and making for their outside toilet where I could allow the tears to spill out without embarrassment, and then eventually pulling myself together and coming into the kitchen to help dry the dishes. This was not an isolated occurrence, but seemed to be repeated day in and day out for weeks and months.

School was a particular trauma, not because I was unable to do the work but because my ears were more attuned to Scottish accents, and I couldn't understand a single word anybody said. Predictably, this got me into trouble on more than one occasion. Despite all that, I actually enjoyed the school environment. My first teacher there was a man who had an intense love of the natural world. He must have had a beehive in the school grounds, as to this day I still remember him taking us all out to sit quietly on the grass while he showed us a swarm of bees and then set up the process of encouraging the bees into a straw skep from where they could be taken to form a new colony. The actual work in the school was easy for me because I had already done most of it in my previous school, so in that respect I was able to shine, something that probably helped me through that first difficult year. I was awarded the top class prize at the end of the year—the only time ever!—and I still have my inscribed *Observer's Book of Birds* to prove it.

During that period my father came to see me whenever he could, but there were many weeks in between each visit. I later realized that this way of life was not as odd as I thought at the time, and many children of missionaries have experienced the same thing. Looking back, though, I think my childhood intuitions about it were correct, and it is not something I could ever recommend or even justify. Though my parents would probably never have seen it this way, there can be no doubt that it did irreparable damage to me as a child. The one enormous advantage it did give me in later years was when I found myself serving as a chairperson for Children's Hearings (part of the Scottish legal system which deals with those under 18 who offend and who are offended against—roughly equivalent to Family Courts in other parts of the world). I am sure that my understanding of all the possible consequences of uprooting a child out of a family to put them into care was significantly informed by my own childhood experience.

On her return from Canada, my father took me to meet my mother. In those days, transatlantic travel was a major enterprise, and it took her five days on an ocean liner, which on its arrival dropped anchor in the deep water of the Firth of Clyde, far out from the port of Greenock. My father had made a special effort and written to the port authorities and we were given tickets to go out on the tugboat to meet the large liner—and my mother. But we did not go back to my childhood home. In the year my mother had been in Canada, my dad must, at some point unknown to me, have packed everything up and moved it all to the northeast of England, where our new home was to be. From now on, my parents were going to be working together in the north of England, leading children's missions in churches during the winter and beach missions in the summer.

Soulmates

This discontinuity in my own family experience has encouraged me as an adult to try to understand what it means to be part of a family, and how faith is nurtured—or indeed strangled—in that context. Throughout the remaining years of my childhood, I always felt only pain and contradiction in my birth family, something that really began to be turned around only in my teens, when I started to talk with John. I had known him on and off since I was about ten years old: our respective families had met while we were both enrolled in a training course on how to ride our cycles, organized by the local police. At that time, he was just one of twenty or thirty others, and was of no significant interest at all to me. But by the time I was seventeen, I had begun to look at people differently, and John and I found in each other real soulmates. Once we became friends, we talked endlessly about everything, couldn't get enough of each other's company, and eventually our friendship blossomed into a real love affair.

Against all the odds, I had continued to explore Christian belief, and my other great passion at this time was to find effective ways of sharing my faith with my contemporaries. My own belief had been kept alive largely through reading the Bible, and reflecting on the Jesus I encountered there, who was radical and seemed to have something to say to the issues that most concerned me—global and social, as well as internal and personal. By contrast, the majority of adults around me (especially the Christians) were mostly cynical and world weary, believing in a theoretical sort of way that things could change, but with no real expectation that they would. I suppose my parents bucked that trend, but all the other things that were going on in my home life did not allow me to see that at the time. As John and I shared our hopes and aspirations, we had a growing ambition to see where our journey together might go if we took God at face value. What we called "guidance" was a big topic in our generation—finding out what God might want us to do with our lives. Expressed in that way, I feel I know less about it now than I thought I did then—though I do know that I've journeyed with God in the meantime. Back in the 1960s, I knew the formula, but reality often contradicts theory.

When John and I decided to marry, we discovered role reversal before the phrase had been coined. By now I was working in medical technology and supporting John, who was studying theology at university. In some of the church circles we knew, both of these things were viewed with suspicion as a slippery slope that would lead to an inevitable loss of faith. It was sometimes hard to know which was the more disapproved of—the theology, or the idea that a man would be dependent on his wife! It was certainly hard going economically, and our budget was continually on a shoestring. But we were dedicated to discovering what it meant to pursue life with God at the center of our relationship.

Even then, we were conscious of the need for community to be a central part of spirituality, and though we lived only briefly in a rented farm cottage just a few miles from the university in Aberdeen, where John was a student, we set about putting our own stamp on it, turning it into a real home that would reflect who we were and who we wanted to become. We very quickly realized what a valuable resource our kitchen table was. We regularly invited friends and acquaintances to join us in sharing simple food. These times were infused with stimulating dialogue and conversation. We laughed and enjoyed one another's company. We explored the meaning of life and faith in a safe context—a process that was shaping who we would become.

During this time, our first son Andrew was born, and then after graduation we left the northeast of Scotland and headed for the industrial northwest of England, to Manchester University. Although at this time John was the one doing the actual studying for a degree, the whole enterprise even then was quite self-consciously about the two of us together. Our embryonic understanding of marriage from the start was partnership, and it was only much later that we realized that not everyone saw things the same way. Christians in particular were supposed to live in certain stereotyped ways, to most of which we never conformed—not because we were nonconformists in any committed sense, but just because these expectations rarely seemed to match what was possible in our circumstances. One plumb line of spiritual progress was for Christian partners to spend time reading the Bible together, but we never did have much success at that. Imagining that, with a degree in theology, he should know more than me, I would ask, "What do you think, John?" in response to which he—not wanting to impose his ideas on me—would say, "Well, what do you think?" Not surprisingly, this discussion never got us very far. But we stuck to the challenge, and John succeeded in obtaining his Ph.D. in record time. His subject—an ancient heresy called Gnosticism—was little-known at the time, but it was to have a profound influence on the rest of our lives, as the same kind of ideas emerged shortly afterwards in the guise of New Age spirituality, which is of course the cultural context into which Christians today are called to minister. Perhaps we were learning more about guidance than we realized.

You might expect that, with all this preparation, we would be ready for God to let us loose on some real project. The reality was that economics were rapidly changing in Britain. No longer could someone with qualifications be sure of a job, and we were the first group of graduates to experience what has become the norm for many nowadays. However, with my usual practical slant I said to John, "Well, you had better write what you've been learning in an accessible way for us ordinary people, and make good use of the time that way." This throwaway suggestion provided the impetus to John to start writing—and since then he's never been able to stop. Our stories are, of course, intimately interconnected with each other's, and readers who are interested in such things might compare John's early writings on the Bible with his most recent book, *The McDonaldization of the Church*, and realize just how profoundly his outlook on life has also been changed by the stories that I am sharing here in this book.[2] At the time, though, he was applying for jobs and we repeatedly went through the same cycle of elation, expectation, disappointment and back to square one. Of course we prayed through all this. Was God deaf? Had we learned so much and understood nothing of guidance? Were we missing some obvious link? Then at last, reassurance came with the brown envelope on the doormat. John was offered a teaching position at Stirling University, back in Scotland.

Down the Mine Shaft

We hastened north, sure in our hearts that God really was dependable. We had a new job, new house, new town and—the icing on the cake—a new baby was on the way. It was worthwhile trusting God through it all: we had not been let down! But then, like a bolt from the blue, our world was shattered.

Overnight things turned upside down for us. We couldn't believe it. Our baby daughter died, and we were devastated. How could this be part of God's plan? We had lived in our new location for little more than a year and had a limited number of friends. Yes, we had a church, but we found that people there and elsewhere walked round us as though on eggshells. They were totally incapable of reaching out to us—or, perhaps, we were so low that we simply couldn't be reached. Was it too hard for them? It was grossly painful for us. But the one certainty was that God was with us—if this had not been the case, we would definitely have drowned. Personally I felt as though I had plummeted down a mine shaft. I sat at the bottom in the damp mud unable to move for a very long time. Not just months, more like years—several of them.

I find it very hard to identify exactly what enabled me to move on eventually. The truth is that there were probably several things in combination. There's no doubt about it that John and I were each other's best help. The relationship and partnership that was being forged in those early years was severely tested, but something of real value was being formed because it was still there after the fire. Even though we still couldn't make a particularly good success of Bible study together, we knew how to pray together. Perhaps that's because prayer is partly conversation and we had always been supremely good at talking together. And, of course, another part of conversation is also listening. The "we" at this time wasn't just John and me. "We" was the two of us and Andrew our son, who by now was five years old. I remember how profoundly moved and comforted we were when praying as usual shortly after the death of our daughter. John prayed, I prayed, and I don't think we had any expectation that our son would be able to join in—it seemed from a mere adult's perception just too hard a thing to do (perhaps because we were finding it difficult for ourselves). But Andrew prayed quite unselfconsciously with us, so "we" was the three of us: already we were discovering new models of being family for ourselves that would enrich our lives in the days to come.

Certainly, starting to look outside ourselves was a significant step. I can remember being horrified watching terrible slaughter and maiming of children on television. I can't even remember which war it was—but it cut through my pain, as I saw other people's devastation. At least I was moving. Another significant influence was a gift of recordings of Handel's *Messiah*. I listened to those over and over again. The words "surely he has borne our griefs and carried our sorrows" (Isaiah 53:4) became infused with a new meaning and the words and familiar music became a means of inner healing. The process was long, and the struggle was definitely uphill.

Our trust in one another eventually led to the birth of Mark, our second son. I had great difficulty believing that he could survive until he arrived strong and healthy, and thereafter the daily care of him itself became a gradual healing process. It wasn't until he was a few months old that I became aware that I could begin to feel again. This child had certainly brought about a miracle. I remember one day our neighbor, who was a nurse, remarking, "It's extraordinary—it's like all three of you are having this baby." We'd shared the pain and now we shared the healing.

Unexpected Encounters

Not so long after that, John was chairing a local group that brought together a variety of churches, and proposed that for his year of office they should embark on some kind of mission focus in which the stronger churches might lend their support to the smaller ones. So we all got involved, and I was part of a group who were to do "something artistic" to present the gospel. I donned a clown outfit for the first time, and found it was enormous fun. I had the very simple task of handing out flyers. Normally, trying to do this in the street is a very good way to become totally invisible to everyone else, for people in Scotland don't usually want to receive bits of paper from total strangers. But dressed as a clown I found that people came and asked me for whatever I had. Everyone wanted my brochures, and I was excited by this. Suddenly I realized that roles had been reversed again: the space had been created for people to ask, instead of being told. I instantly liked this, and knew I would have to explore it more fully. It was only when I came to reflect on it some years later that it dawned on me that this is exactly what Jesus had recommended when he sent out the seventy (Luke 10:1-12).

There had been a small group of clowns performing at that particular event, led by Philip Noble, a priest in the Scottish Episcopal Church. At the end of the day he said to me, "Olive, I'm leading a weekend of workshops on clowning in the near future: I think you should come." I will always be grateful that Philip said that. I think it was a moment of discernment on his part, and in due course I went—not very happily, as it happened. For a start, I now had a baby daughter as well, and didn't really want to leave her for a whole weekend. But my family insisted, and so I found myself in a more-or-less rundown church hall in Leith, which at the time was one of the seedier parts of Edinburgh. On the Friday night of the course, we watched *Parable*, a film that had been produced for the 1964 New York World Fair. This film has exercised such a significant influence in the development of my theology of clowning that it requires more comprehensive analysis, and we will come back to it in chapter 8, where I also present some in-depth reflection on my own story. The Saturday morning after watching the film, we learned about makeup and simple skills like juggling, before taking "the Plunge," which is clown jargon for your first trip outside in costume. Philip led and the rest of us were the backup. We headed straight to the nearest shopping mall, and I couldn't believe how quickly this bunch of oddities who had never met each other before were so suddenly transformed into a supportive group. We could have sat and listened to any number of series of Bible teaching addresses for weeks and not learned so much—it was staggering. After unpacking what we had learned and then putting something together for the church service the next morning, the weekend ended with worship, followed by church lunch and then home.

On my return, I enthused to all my church friends about this experience. Their faces were an absolute picture. They didn't need to say anything, but they were obviously thinking, "Just what you'd expect of her. Whatever will she do next?" So I carried on with "normal" life, cleaning the house, caring for children, answering the phone and all the other hundreds of executive decisions that every full-time parent makes every day. In between, I reflected on why, how and where this clowning might fit into my life. This period in my life really was my Arabian experience (see Galatians 1:17). Then it registered: I could tell a story. Isn't that what Jesus had done—telling stories and asking questions? But which story? Well, my own of course, for that was the one I knew best.

Conversations with "The Voice"

So I started to craft my story in a way that would be accessible to others. After many tellings, I have come to appreciate what listeners find humorous—because they laugh! In what has become my classic trademark way of sharing this story, I usually put the makeup on my face and don my clown clothes while I am talking. I always tell the story in the form of a conversation between myself and someone who is not there, but whom I call "The Voice." I don't immediately articulate that this is God—part of good storytelling and clowning is its non-prescriptive nature, leaving the hearers to work things out for themselves. I begin from where I found myself following the death of my daughter, desolate and forsaken, feeling as though I was lost in a bottomless mine shaft. And from that point on, the story typically continues pretty much like this:

One day, in that cold damp place, it's as if I heard a voice saying, "Olive, we have to get you out of here."

"Easier said than done," I quipped. It didn't even strike me as unusual that I was speaking to The Voice. The struggle to get out of that pit was like climbing up a sheer rock face with precious little to get a foothold or a handhold into. But slowly, inch by inch, and eventually with an almighty shove (and I use the word "Almighty" advisedly), I was out into the daylight. I could hardly believe it; then slowly I started to unfold like a tiny crocus in the spring sunshine.

It must have been some time after that when I heard laughter. I looked for the source but could see nothing. It came again. I looked more carefully, but still nothing was obvious. The chuckling continued—and ever so slowly I realized that it was me who was laughing. As the enormity of what was happening dawned on me, I burst into a full-throated explosion of laughter. Truly I had never expected to laugh like that again. Deep joy swelled up from within my being and spilled helplessly over the edge. "Thank you, God," I said, from the bottom of my heart. You, the reader, must decide whether the next thing I said was quite so sane. "If there's anything," I said with abandon, "anything you'd like me to do— you just have to say." I was totally unprepared for the response.

"Wonderful. At the moment I'm looking for a clown."

I knew enough of my Bible to know that God doesn't say things like that. "I was thinking more along the lines of maybe becoming a social worker, or a teacher, or even something to do with computers. I'm still young enough to retrain, you know."

"Yes, of course, I know all that. But to tell you the truth, I have millions of people with those skills who are already working most effectively in my kingdom. But there are not so many who are ready to volunteer to be clowns."

"But haven't you got a whole church full of clo . . .?" Whoops! I was in this up to my neck. "Well, OK, but if I end up looking stupid you'll know it's your fault!"

"Fine. I can handle that. Here's some new makeup for you. Go on, take it—it's a gift."

"Thanks. I always like new makeup. But hang on a minute. Where did you get this stuff? I'm not sure this is my color. Haven't you read any good glossy magazines lately? You're supposed to try it out on your jawline and find a color that blends with your skin tone. This stuff is more like plaster in color, and looks like it would do about the same job—fill the cracks."

"No, it's the perfect color. Crisp, clean white. Sign of a brand new start. Try it on. Everyone who asks me for help gets this brand new start."

So, cautiously, I applied it and thought to myself, "I look more like I belong in a shroud."

But The Voice was still speaking: "Now take the powder and fix it."

"Fix it! You mean I'll stay like this?"

"I always fix it. Didn't I say: everyone who asks me gets a brand new start, and I never change the ground rules. Now come on, I've got some more makeup to add to your collection."

Dubiously I opened the next box. Lime green, scarlet, orange, aquamarine, purple—every color you could imagine, in their zaniest hues. Certainly not subtle. I cautiously picked up one of the new brushes, dipped it in the lime green and painted one eyebrow. Hmmm. Orange for the other? Why be the same? Nose? Red, of course. The first attempt produced a huge red nose which I discovered was not a good idea! A moment's thought should have told me that being a nosy parker can lead to unpleasant results. A similar result with the first scarlet mouth—too big. It would have been good if I had appreciated in advance what James was saying about how a big mouth can get you into a lot of trouble (James 3:6). These days, my clown makeup includes quite a petite mouth. In fact I frequently take it a step further and use silent mime.

The face was surely coming together. But I had no idea what to wear. The new face definitely called for new clothes, and since the high street shops had nothing obvious to offer, I was forced to go back to basics.

Out came my sewing machine, and a visit to the fabric shop unearthed the most unexpectedly luminous pink material hiding among the bridal collection. This provided the inspiration for a baggy shirt and pants. Further searching uncovered black velvet studded with sequins of every color—gold, silver, metallic red, blue, green and purple. This made a wonderful tailcoat, which unfortunately had no sleeves because I hadn't bought enough material. But just wait—the best-dressed clergy will all be wearing this before we've gone much further into the 21st century! They sometimes take a while to catch up, but when they do, remember that you first heard it here.

I started to turn out the cupboards and drawers at home, searching for long-forgotten birthday and Christmas presents. I found the ideal pair of socks—black and red horizontal stripes which some dear friend had fondly imagined someone might wear. Of course, the socks had found their way to the back of the drawer, but now they would be the very thing—they would clash beautifully with all the rest. A tie made of pearls, a shiny beaded belt bought in a street market in the Philippines, an old pair of 1970s-style pink boots, and white gloves. It is amazing what can be uncovered in the average house!

"Well God, what do you think?"

"I think you should book a hair appointment."

"A what? You surprise me. I didn't know you were interested in such trivial matters."

"Have you forgotten? I've counted the hairs on your head before today."

So off I went to visit my usual hairdresser. "What can we do for you today, madam? How about something more exciting than a blue rinse? Pink? Green? Yellow? Orange? Fuchsia? Mmmm?"

"How about them all together? I've a new friend I'd like to impress," I said.

"On your head be it," quipped my astonished hairdresser.

(At this point in a presentation I would usually invite the audience to humor me: when I say "curtains down" they close their eyes, and before I say "curtains up" for them to open their eyes again, I don my multi-colored wig and proceed to titivate it with a two-foot-long comb).

"Well, God. What do you really reckon?"

"Just my style. Will you do me the honor of coming out for a walk with me?" said God, holding open my front door.

Seeing the World the Way God Sees It

The story continues by taking the hearers on an imaginary journey with me as a clown. What would it be like to step outside my front door? What would the neighbors think? The comments I might typically make on the people in my community are common to us all. My reflections are a way of expressing the struggle I have with how I find things in real life, and my attempt to have integrity with the teachings of Jesus.

In response to God's invitation, I therefore very cautiously peeped round the door, desperately hoping my nearest neighbor wasn't in his garden. After all, he was at the time on the editorial team of a well-known daily newspaper.

"How about we walk across by the river?" I ventured, hoping that we would not meet too many people in that direction.

"Yes, let's go and check out· my creation," said God. But before long, even that began to get just a bit unsettling, as God asked about a red-and-white thing in the river. "What's that?"

"Oh, that's a traffic cone."

"And those?"

"Cola cans. Don't you drink cola, God?"

Slowly the point of all these questions registered with me, so I hastily set the record straight: "Oh, none of my family put that rubbish there. We recycle all our stuff."

I decided it was time to move on. "Let's go across to the other side of the sports field and I'll show you some of the prettiest gardens you could imagine," said I, thinking to impress even the Almighty. As we reached the house on the street corner, the curtains seemed to move voluntarily, although there was no breeze and the windows were tight shut.

"Who lives in there?" asked God.

"Oh, I don't actually know her name, you understand."

"Have you ever invited her to coffee?"

"Well no, I'm pretty sure she wouldn't come."

"How do you know if you haven't asked her?"

Fortunately for me, just then there was a great commotion further down the street. A man I knew came hurrying out of his house closely followed by an airborne suitcase, spreading its contents far and wide in the process. Then came a string of adjectives so highly colored you could just about see them, and then—oh dear—his wife. "Not the best time to introduce you, God."

"How about we go back to your place?" countered God, acknowledging my obvious embarrassment.

"Yes, I could certainly do with some coffee, if not something stronger."

It was still mid-afternoon, so I settled for coffee, and while we were waiting for the kettle to boil, God made a very astute observation: "Olive, you didn't use all the colors in your paint box."

"Well, I wouldn't want to overdo things."

"Will you trust me? Close your eyes."

What else does one say and do in the presence of God? I did as I was asked, and felt the cold, wet bristles of the fine brush touching my eyelid and trickling on to my left cheek, and then across the other way. The same across both my eyes and cheeks.

"Now take a look," said God holding the mirror up for me to see. I lifted it up. I hesitated: what I saw was a black cross over each eye, in classic clown style: "I'm not sure it's an improvement."

But God continued, "From now on, I want you to see the world the way I see it—I want you to see things through the cross."

"Will that make a difference?"

"I certainly hope so."

"Do you mean the mess in the river, by any chance?"

"Yes."

"The old woman behind the curtains? The one who probably drinks gin all the time?"

"Her too."

Looking quizzically at God, and not a little unsure of what it might all mean, I found myself asking, "You don't really mean the family who were fighting?"

"I most certainly do."

"Everything?"

"You've got it."

It was only as I reflected on all this later that I appreciated what it meant for there to be no "no-go" areas for God, and that this clowning business would eventually affect my entire lifestyle.

Then God repeated the invitation: "I'm going out again. Are you coming with me—see what difference the cross can make?"

"Well, maybe there's some family business I need to do first. I really need to go and see my granny."

"Don't worry, Olive, I'll look after your granny. Are you coming with me?"

"How about I just go to the shops and buy a new pair of jeans first: I want to look my best . . . well, you never know—we might get asked to a party or something."

"Really, I like you just the way you are. Are you coming with me?"

"Well, I'll just go by the bank first. . . ."

"Don't worry, my friend, I always carry cash. Are you coming?"

Those hearing my story who have some Bible knowledge might recognize that I am playing here with the story in John 21, where Jesus challenges Peter by asking him three times in a row, "Do you love me?" But it's of no consequence that not everyone listening to me will recognize that allusion. It forms a suitable point on which to conclude, inviting others to engage their stories with mine, and reflect on the challenge of following Jesus in today's world.

From where I was beginning back then, I knew that there really were no other options but to respond positively to such an invitation. I had already started on my journey from brokenness to healing, and I now needed to explore what other transformations could be brought about by the power of God's Spirit.

Chapter 2

I've Been There Too, Valentine

This dramatic encounter with God definitely changed the direction of my life, but still the everyday things of life had to be orchestrated. When the doorbell rang one morning just after breakfast, I knew it would be one of my friends calling to give my daughter Alethea a ride to nursery school along with her own child. Edith had the capacity to look bright and cheerful no matter what time of day it might be, and I can't remember ever seeing her without immaculate makeup, even before nine in the morning. When she bounced around on the doorstep with a glint in her eye, that warned me that she had a bright idea. At the time, she was the art teacher at school, and she said, "I've just had a brain wave. What if I was to do a project on clowns, and you could come dressed in all your finery?" The way she said it, it was more of a statement than a question. "The children would love to paint you!"

"I bet they would," I thought, but because she had been such a good friend, helping me out in so many ways, I agreed, even though I had real misgivings. My son Mark was also a student at the same school, and I wondered what he might think about his mother turning up dressed as a clown—not to mention what the other teachers would think. Would I for ever be labeled as "that crazy woman"?

Well, I went to school in my clown outfit and, doing the only thing I knew how—because, remember, these were really early days for me—I tiptoed along the corridor to the art room, heart pounding, mouth going dry, and peeped into the room. Someone spotted me right away, and I jumped back, but by the time I peeped round the door again all eyes were focused to see why the door was partly open, and speculating about what might happen next. What a reception! We had great fun, and for me it was instant affirmation. School had certainly never been like this for me when I was a child, and as the morning went on I found myself really enjoying it all. The lids came off the paint boxes, and eager young hands grabbed the brushes to take a great dollop of their favorite color in order to explore "the colors of life."

The Name Game

We were obviously enjoying ourselves so much that no one realized that the noise level in the classroom had risen to a higher than usual number of decibels. And then it happened. Suddenly, framed in the glass panel in the door was the face of . . . yes, you've got it—the head teacher. How I wished I could do a vanishing trick, but since I didn't know how to accomplish that, it had to be the next best thing. I remember thinking to myself, "If I stand absolutely still, I won't be seen." Whenever I tell this today, everyone falls about laughing because of the absurdly bright clothes that I wear, and the very idea of them acting as camouflage is just too ridiculous for words. Of course, I was spotted right away. The head teacher came straight over to me, and oddly enough I found myself wanting to do what all schoolchildren do in such circumstances—looking at the floor, which had suddenly become an object of great fascination to me. "Hello, clown," she said, "it's wonderful that you've come to school. What's your name?" Oh, dear, if only I could have anticipated that question, I would have given it some thought in advance. It was, after all, a fairly obvious place to start making small talk with a clown. I really was more of a novice than I thought. I scratched my head, and in an instant the scratching of the wiry multicolored wig I was wearing enabled me to blurt out, "Rainbow."

"Well, that's a beautiful name. We do hope you will enjoy your day with us."

With that, the moment of potential disaster was thankfully over. My heart rate gradually returned to normal, but I felt slightly out of sync for the rest of the time, enjoyable though it was.

When I got home, I knew that I needed to reflect on why such a simple question had unsettled me so much and so easily. As I thought about it, I realized I'd done what all children do when they are threatened: they reach out to grab their parent's hand. I had subconsciously reached out for my mentor's hand—Philip Noble. His clown name at that time was Rainbow. Oh dear, I truly felt as though I had stolen something very precious. I knew I would have to address this. But where do clowns get their names from? I thought and thought, and scribbled and doodled like mad—and even prayed—but nothing I managed to come up with had the feeling of being a really good solution. Then I realized that I didn't need to tackle this alone, and so in one quiet moment I caught my husband unawares and posed the question to him: "John, what would be a good choice for a clown name?"

"Oh, I don't know," he replied, perhaps predictably.

"Well, you work in a university—you're paid to think!"

"Leave it with me, I'll consider it."

I kid you not, it was fully two years later when I got the response. Totally out of the blue, he said, "Valentine." If it had been February 14 I might not have been too surprised by this—but in November?

"Well, what about Valentine?" I enquired.

"For a clown name, of course."

"Oh, hang on a minute: it's all right for you to call me Valentine, but not every one—and then only once a year. If I go out not only dressed in my clown gear, but also telling people my name is Valentine, whatever will people think?"

"Oh well, it was just an idea."

Knowing that it could take another two years for him to have another one, I thought I had better do some serious reflecting, and so I turned with a plea to God: "I thought I asked for help. This is not one of your better suggestions!"

"Rubbish," came the response, "it's the perfect solution. Now you can tell everyone that God loves you—and them. It's a perfect description: God's love in action."

I just had to trust that God knew the score, though I made a mental note never to ask a theologian a question if I was in a hurry for an answer. So Valentine became my clown name, and in a more significant way than I anticipated, the process of actually finding a name had become another stage on my journey of self-discovery, something that in spiritual terms could be equated to baptism or bat mitzvah—or, in the words of Ephesians 4:13, growing up into maturity, "the measure of the full stature of Christ." Naming my clown owned my calling, and with the benefit of hindsight I'm glad that John had such a significant part in it because he is the one who has supported and encouraged me when others had no idea where I might be going.

Telling the Story

Finding a name also gave me the confidence to continue the process of making my story accessible to other people. I didn't immediately realize that I was doing what every generation before me had done, by taking their life experience and handing it on to the next generation. This is the way that tried and tested life skills have been passed down in most cultures from time immemorial. We all have the potential within us to be good storytellers. Our own journey is unique and therefore we are the ones best able to share it. In the process of sharing, we reflect and discover much about ourselves. Even so, it was with great trepidation that I first told my own story. But I quickly found that people would come and say what seemed to me the most amazing things—like "That's just where I am . . ." or " . . .where my husband/daughter/sister/friend is right now." It wasn't that they had necessarily had exactly the same experience, but the apparent injustice or inexplicably tragic nature of life left them struggling with the same questions as I had wrestled with, and as often as not making a similar emotional response.

In the process, I began to discover the particular things that would connect especially with a certain sort of audience. For instance, when in telling my story I talk about God suggesting that I need a new hairdo and I act surprised, I might use a phrase like, "I didn't know you were interested in trivial things like that," and go on to imagine God responding with something like, "Have you forgotten I've got all those hairs numbered?" For those with a biblical background, that apparently throwaway remark will immediately connect with Jesus' words in Matthew 10:30, "Even the hairs of your head are all counted." It will reinforce for them the simple everyday application of the Bible story, just as it may also trigger some memories of a personal application of that verse to them in the past, and be all the more helpful as a result. Those without that background will not be especially disadvantaged, but this kind of casual remark may easily help to open them to the possibility that God can be interested even—or especially—in the "trivia" of our lives. In the process, it will perhaps encourage them to ask questions that will take them further on their spiritual search.

Telling a story is different from reading a story from a set script. It demands an awareness of how the hearers are receiving and interacting with the story. Storytellers, clowns and artists of all types learn to read their audience's body language and expression. If you think about it, we all do this unconsciously. We step back from someone who has a threatening pose, for example. So when I see a child itching to look in my paint box, I might say, "Would you like to choose a color for my eyebrows?" Or maybe, "Can you paint? Would you like to paint my eyebrows?" Children often interrupt and give me advice. This flexibility obviously carries its own risk, but being vulnerable is an important aspect of clown ministry, a topic that deserves fuller exploration in a later chapter.

To be given this sort of invitation is usually a very affirming experience for a curious child, and creates a memory that they will probably take with them through the rest of life. In the same way, the other children will be sitting on the edge of their seats wishing they had been brave enough to volunteer. Quite often this kind of interaction will provide me with the very precious gift of a comment that would be inappropriate for me to make spontaneously—like "My mom uses that" or, as one child once said in church in a penetrating voice so that everyone could hear, "I think they've turned the service off this morning." Even those who gave no further thought to my clowning will have had plenty to reflect on from that remark.

More often, though, the responses my story evokes will be related to personal pain. I remember a woman in her eighties who came to me after I had spoken at a coffee club in a hotel in the east of Scotland, and with a trembling voice told me how she had lost her first child during World War I. Her husband had been away in the army, she had had no close family support, and that kind of experience wasn't talked about in either her community or the church. Somehow, whatever happened as she listened to me created a safe space for her to talk about the pain of the past. I could, and did, weep with her and then we prayed and committed her and her child to God. It was worth being there just for that one person, though I have to admit that I was shocked that someone could have carried that burden for more than half a century without others in the Christian community sharing it. Then I recalled my own experience, and realized that there must be many thousands of people in exactly the same situation.

All Places Great and Small

Other days, I find myself working before huge crowds. One such event, about five years after I had started clowning, was in 1991 at the Scottish Christian Resources Exhibition held in the Scottish Exhibition and Conference Center in Glasgow. The final event of the three-day program included a number of groups who had played a part in workshops held throughout the day, and who came together for a huge celebration of worship to mark the close of the exhibition. It's not often that church people get to work with state-of-the-art equipment, but on this occasion we did.

Dance is one of the other visual arts that I have explored in the context of worship in church, and it seemed natural for me to bring clowning and dance together. The song that was used was Graham Kendrick's "Shine, Jesus, Shine." A group of dancers wore brightly colored dresses and danced the whole song interpretatively. Valentine came wandering in clumsily, picked out by a spotlight, and was so evidently attracted by the music and the color that she tried desperately to join in. But she was unable quite to master the movements, until the third verse, beginning with the lyrics, "Lord, I come to your awesome presence . . ." In the course of this verse, the clown knelt at the feet of one dancer, who moved her body into the shape of the cross, shedding light on to the kneeling clown, and then as Valentine rose she found herself able to dance the final chorus in unison with the dancers, transformed into a perfect dancer through an encounter with Christ.

It was very exciting and moving to be part of this event, but at the end a social worker who had been struggling with some crisis in her life came and said, "That could have been me at the foot of that cross." It was as if she also was oblivious of the crowds and she met the living Christ in a new way. A priest who was also there said to me, "I think when you clown it's like pulling back the curtain and making a space for God to step in." It was only some time later, when I was looking at photographs of the event, that I noticed that projected behind the stage there had been a massive cross streaming out light on the almost insignificant little figures in the dance. What a beautiful expression of the body of Christ working together—dance, mime, music, clowning, lighting technicians, sound engineers, all working together as God intended the body of Christ to function!

One of the great strengths of the creative and expressive arts is the open-ended nature of the communication. It is not dogmatic, but rather leaves people of any age free to engage with it in whatever way might happen to be relevant to their life circumstances at that particular moment in time. It is not my job to work out all the possible interpretations or understandings of what I do: that is the work of the Holy Spirit. My prayer is that my work will always be in tune with God's Spirit. Such creative presentation allows people to ask questions, and doesn't even attempt to give all the answers. I suppose I am happy with this because that is how Jesus worked: he told stories and asked questions, unlike many Christians who prefer to preach sermons and give answers. It's a pity that most of the answers we frequently give are to questions only the preacher has been asking.

For me, this whole process of exploring the arts was in a real sense the completion of my education. Brought up in the United Kingdom, having attended school and college in England and Scotland, I had been trained in an educational system that only explored certain areas of human experience. Or, to be more precise, experience had never been explored at all, particularly in the kind of scientific field where I had previously worked, and in which feelings, emotions, trust, and creative capacity had been neglected, if not positively discouraged. The churches I had known adopted exactly the same attitude, and though I had a Christian up-bringing, the models I had been given for how faith might be expressed in daily life had never included these areas of creative potential. So in many ways I came to it all like a child in a room full of new toys. Children don't usually get one toy out, play with it, put it away and get another out: they spread the whole lot all over the room and move from one to another, playing with them all, and often doing it all at once. A jigsaw is as likely to become ballast for a train, while a baby pram becomes a good wheelbarrow, a mirror becomes a pond for the ducks, and the boxes they all came in might easily be used to create the farmyard or a boat to sit in and paddle around, depending on size. I found that when I started to play for the first time, I was on a very fast learning curve. Many of the books on clowning talk about "finding the child within ourselves," and though I didn't realize it at the time, that is what I was doing. Perhaps play acted as a catalyst in my inner healing. Is that why children heal faster than adults, I wonder?

The Masks We Wear

It was while I was playing one summer morning in 1992 at the Graduate Theological Union in Berkeley, in northern California, that I discovered (or rediscovered) the joys of having fun with plaster of Paris. This time it was in the form of plaster bandaging, of the kind used to set broken bones. We made masks on one another and then two people acted out the story of the conversation that Cain had with God after he had murdered his brother Abel (Genesis 4:1-16). I immediately felt comfortable with this medium, and once I was back home in Scotland I began to play with it on my own.

Shortly after this, John accepted an invitation to speak on the figure of Abraham at a major Christian event. Like many such invitations, it seemed like a good idea at the time but as the occasion drew nearer he was really struggling with what to say about him. Abraham can seem quite a good guy if you read the book of Hebrews (11:8-19), but the story looks a bit different if viewed from the perspectives of his children or his sexual partners. As a way of working through this, the idea was born of making masks of the different expressions of the people in the story. This turned out to be a different sort of sermon preparation and exegesis. Maybe you could describe it as emotional exegesis. What comes out of the stories when you imagine being a child who is threatened by their brutish father? Or a wife whose husband says, "Pretend you are my sister" when passing through hostile territory, and then discovers that the king of that land fancies you and puts you in his harem? Or a woman who becomes pregnant by her master at his wife's suggestion and is then turned out with her son when the same wife gives birth to her own child? If this man and his family lived next door, you would be reporting him to the social services or the police, not praising him as a model of spiritual virtue.

These cannot be pictures of behavior to emulate, but rather challenges to our lifestyles in our own culture. Why are so many children abused and women violated as we begin the third millennium? Of course, there is good news in the Bible story, for

God saw Hagar's misery, Isaac's terror, Sarah's predicament and even Abraham's ambition, and stepped in to empower the weak ones and challenge the abuser and invite all to embark on a spiritual journey. This is indeed good news for us today. As it turned out, it became good news for many who heard the resultant sermon at that event. At least one perpetrator of sexual abuse came into the open, confessed and was helped through the appropriate courses the law had to take, while many who were violated and in abusive relationships were empowered to take the first steps to their own healing.

As I write this, I have just met a woman who is now heading up an organization called "Set Free," whose aim is to enable victims of abuse to find freedom—and on that very night she had taken the first step to escape from abuse by her husband, who was a Christian minister. This is almost ten years on, and in the intervening period significant numbers of such people have crossed our paths who say they heard that message, and it made a difference. The point I want to make is that if a more "normal," bookish mode of exegesis had been followed, those issues would almost certainly never have been raised, because bookish methods of Bible reading ask abstract questions and produce abstract answers.

I could write a book of stories on mask-making alone. I have led many workshops where people make masks on one another. One of its attractions is that it is a fun thing to do, and adults don't often do messy things just for fun. It's also very relaxing because you just have to lie back and enjoy the experience and discover in the process what it's like not to be able to see or speak as the mask gradually takes shape. Taking the mask off has been described as being born, transformation, releasing, fun—but the best comment I ever heard was from an African American who was in a class I was teaching at Fuller Seminary in Pasadena, California. He admitted, "All my life I have wanted to be white. The white people seemed to have all the good jobs, the best houses, the biggest cars, and the most promising opportunities. But you know what I found out today? I've seen myself white—

and I don't like it. I now know what it means to be really free."
Unfortunately I can't convey to you here the intonation of excitement that was in his voice. You will have to imagine that for yourself, but I can tell you he was pretty animated. Then he said, with a glint of mischief in his eye, "An' I'm gonna take this home and put it on when I go in, an' I'm gonna shout to my wife, 'Hi honey, guess what I've been doing? Come and have a kiss!'"

Of course, this kind of understanding all comes out in the reflection afterwards. It's crucial in the use of the arts—whether drama, mime, mask-making, or anything else—that you allow time to unpack what has been taking place. That in itself makes the occasion open-ended, because it takes control away from the person who is up at the front. Most clergy and other leaders find this enormously threatening, because we like to be in control. The mistaken view is that if the leader is not in control, everything else is out of control. But what really happens is that when the leader is not in control, others are empowered. That is at the heart of the gospel.

I remember leading a mask-making workshop at Lee Abbey (a retreat center in Devon) some years ago, and one woman insisted she wanted to be there, but would not take part. In a somewhat patronizing tone, she assured me that she already knew all about it because, as she said, "I'm a retired school principal." Fortunately for me, not everyone reacted that way. Another woman spoke with me for a long time after everyone else had gone, and in the end she went off to wrestle with God over a major unresolved issue in her life. I had listened, prayed, talked with her, but in the end she had a choice to make. She came to the worship that night, at which I had set up a cross draped with red silk and a basket at the foot of it, to receive the mask of any who felt they might want to offer this in response to God. When this woman arrived in the room, I think everyone knew that something had happened, before she said anything. The person who had been in so much emotional pain all week was now radiant, and she was one of the first to put her mask in the basket.

I had to wait a bit longer to discover what had been going on with the former school principal—about six months in fact. She wrote and reminded me that she had been the one who refused to make a mask, and explained that since then she had experienced a series of dreams in which she had been plagued by a mask that had the face of her sister imprinted on it. As I began to read, I was a bit alarmed, wondering what I had done, but as I read on I was reassured. She told me that the two of them had fallen out years ago, and hadn't spoken for a very long time, but as a result of this experience she had made contact again and put right whatever there had been between them. She had no need to write to me, for by then I had all but forgotten about her not making a mask on that occasion. I always leave people the freedom to take part or not. Jesus always did this and he is our model. But I am still glad that she told me. It lets me share the story with you, and remind you that we don't always know what part we might be playing in God's work, and we don't need to know all the outcomes—though it is encouraging to discover some of them just now and again.

It also illustrates the capacity the arts have for sowing seeds in people's lives that germinate long after the event. In the normal course of things, we do not remember words for anything like as long as we retain a visual image. The Chinese have a wonderful saying that sums this up well and underlines that, while talking and seeing are both God-given capacities, doing something is an even more powerful catalyst for spiritual and personal growth:

I hear I forget
I see I understand
I do I remember

Chapter 3

Now There Are Two

I think it was the Danish theologian Søren Kierkegaard who talked about "living life forward and reflecting backward." When I came across that phrase it was like a light being switched on for me. There are not too many moments in life when we read or hear something and it articulates for us what, up to that point, we have been unable to put into words. But on reflection, I knew that that was exactly how it had been for me—not just the birth of Valentine the clown, but the whole of my life up to that point and then subsequently, learning to live with Valentine. Most days we just have to get on and live, responding to the opportunities that present themselves in an attitude of prayer—and then later, somewhere down the line in the reflection and the unpacking, we "do theology," as we reflect on our faith, our experience of life and worship, and in the process begin to work out the significance of it all.

I did not at first specifically search for invitations to share the Valentine story. At the start, I don't think it ever occurred to me that anyone else would be very interested in my experience. So I just did what I had always done, and got on with my life. If I had been young and unattached, I may have deliberately chosen to go out and find other clowns, perhaps by attending one of the excellent circus schools that exist around the world. But this was not so easy for me as a wife and mother to three children. Largely through the growing reputation of my husband John, new opportunities opened up for us as a family to become involved in leading weekend events and special seminars for churches of many different denominations. The topics that we found people were interested in were predominantly related to effective sharing of faith and the development of a relevant spirituality for today's lifestyles. In the process of finding something relevant to share, it seemed natural for me to introduce these new forms of communication that I was exploring. As well as the clowning and mask-making that I have already mentioned, I had also started playing with storytelling, dance and visual art.

Out of such informal and low-key events, Valentine eventually received many significant opportunities to explore new horizons—not least through visiting different countries, and in particular by experiencing something of the breadth of the Christian church's diversity, most significantly of all perhaps the non-Western church. These were the people who were not like me. They did not have a white imperial history as part of their baggage. They had not grown up or been educated (if they had had any formal education at all) in the setting of a post-Enlightenment worldview with a strong sense of individualism and over-emphasis on the cognitive in opposition to the relational. This realization only dawned on me gradually, and my discoveries can certainly best be described as a process or journey, though there were a number of significant moments along the way.

One of these was when I first met with Raymond Fung, who at the time was responsible for the Evangelism desk at the World Council of Churches in Geneva. Raymond's personal starting point had been as an industrial evangelist in the sweatshops of Hong Kong. As he shared with me what he called the "Isaiah Vision," I found it to be profoundly illuminating.[3] At roughly this period, my husband John had also eventually found healing from the loss of our daughter, not through clowning but through being invited to chair a committee. The very idea of such a thing will be mind-blowing for many, no doubt. But the group he chaired was an ecumenical committee to be responsible for looking at present-day needs in Scotland in relation to mission and evangelism. So many significant things in relation to the mission of the church were coming together for me all at once. It is interesting that the first thing I was learning was that I didn't know a great deal, and my primary task was to listen to what God was already doing in the world (what theologians call the *missio Dei*). As I did so, it was immediately obvious to me that most of the truly creative initiatives were coming from the Two-thirds World—from people whom we in the West typically imagine to be impoverished. They often are, of course, in economic and financial terms (for much of which we in the West must accept corporate responsibility). But in terms of journeying with God, I have consistently found them to be way out in front.

Creative Clergy

An important encouragement to put some of this experience together in a more comprehensive form came from Bill Buchan, who at the time was minister of Kilwinning Abbey, an ancient place of worship located in a former mining area in southwest Scotland. He was planning a Christmas service based on the traditional Advent crown, and incorporating some materials produced by Christian Aid for use throughout Advent. As one might expect from Christian Aid, these materials were particularly raising issues related to oppression and injustice. What came out of that was one of the most exciting services of which I have ever been a part.

It was significant in the planning of the service that Bill Buchan was a clergy person who did not feel the need to control everybody else. As we talked together in advance about the possibilities, we came up with the idea of a group of clowns interrupting the service at various points. This was hardly an innovation, as it was precisely the traditional role of the clown in churches centuries ago. The Holy Fool of the Middle Ages had the opportunity to say, "Hang on a minute, take a look at yourself: is that really what you think/mean?"

The present church building in Kilwinning stands alongside the ruins of the original abbey, and is in a traditional Presbyterian format, broader than it is long and with pews placed on three sides of the pulpit which is in the center of one of the longer walls. There is a large carpeted dais, a gallery supported by lots of pillars, and a large pipe organ. On the wall facing the pulpit, the main entrance has been tastefully updated with beautiful new clear glass doors leading on to a large porch. This allows the church to remain warm but provides a bright and welcoming space for greeting. Because this service was to be the traditional service on the last Sunday immediately before Christmas Day itself, we piled up huge parcels wrapped in wrapping paper in this area, so that the worshipers' expectations would be heightened even as they arrived. The usual tradition of the Church of Scotland is for every service to begin with the beadle preceding the minister into the church, carrying the Bible and placing it open in a central position—thereby acknowledging the place that is given to the Word of God. On this occasion, that did not take place, and when the minister got to the front he said, "Something's missing this morning: what could it be?" He got the answer in due course: it was the Bible, but no one knew where it was. To great hoots of laughter, one small boy suggested that maybe the beadle had sold it, and Bill was not slow to pick up on this unexpected cue with the comment that, far from being a silly suggestion, that was a pretty good answer because in actual fact the Bible was a very precious book. Just then, two or three clowns came in carrying one of the huge gift-wrapped presents, preceded by another clown with a brush, sweeping the way before them. The thinking behind this was inspired by the part played by John the Baptist in the stories of the first Christmas, inviting the people of Israel to get ready for the coming of Christ, coupled with overtones of the church's regular tradition of the beadle carrying in the scriptures. All this, of course, interrupted what the minister was doing, but when the box arrived and was deposited at the front of the church, he opened up the parcel, with adults as well as children by now straining on the edge of their seats to see what would come out.

You've probably guessed already that inside the box (along with much fancy packaging, balloons and other fun things) was the Bible, which was then ceremoniously taken out and opened to be placed in its usual position. Because of the familiarity of the ritual, in a regular service only a few people might pay any attention at all to the Bible's arrival. But this time, it could hardly be missed, and because clowns had produced it, it was possible for the minister to join in the fun by apparently blowing much dust off it—a visual aid that in itself carried the unspoken prayer that we would all be enabled to hear the old, familiar story with a new clarity of understanding. And so the first carol was sung and the service got under way. But such a lot had happened already.

The second clown interruption was a much more sedate affair—partly because it involved a thin, large, gold box carried carefully in the hands of a very regal-looking jester, processing down the aisle carefully and slowly. She was going slowly because it was her first public appearance as a clown, her "Plunge" as Jangle the Jester, but no one else would ever have guessed as she knelt down and solved the problem of the missing fourth candle for the Advent crown, by producing it from the box.

It was fortuitous that there was to be the baptism of one of the youngest in the congregation that day, a baby boy just a few weeks old. Another clown went to the place where the child's family were waiting, and escorted them and the child into the center of the church. This time, the gift was not in a box, I hasten to add! But the theme was continued, as the child took a central place as an especially appropriate expression, on this day of all days, of God's gifts to us. After the baptism the baby was duly taken on a walk around the church and introduced to the congregation, while the clowns brought in a huge bunch of balloons printed with the logo "God loves you" inside a Valentine heart, and presented them to the family. I'm sure the family are not the only ones who will long remember that service. The carols continued, and the small children formed their tableau of the nativity, which had been well rehearsed and had all the familiar elements of angels struggling to keep their headdresses on, shepherds tripping over their crooks, kings in their grand robes, and so on—the kind of thing that parents have nightmares about in advance, but which bring joy and pleasure to their hearts when they see their children up front carrying off the part.

Barni's Christmas

But how do you fit a sermon in among all this? Of course, for those with "ears to hear," at least a dozen sermons had already been preached, for every element of the service was oozing with significance. But at this point, a dad from the congregation climbed the stairs into the pulpit with his little girl. This was to become their "house" for the mime that followed. He did what many dads in our culture do on Sunday mornings: he settled down to read the paper, while his small daughter looked out of the "window" (over the side of the pulpit). Like most little girls, she knew better than to expect a great response while her dad was reading the paper, but hoped that patience would ultimately pay off. Outside the window, however, there was nothing especially interesting to look at—only the dustbin stuffed full of rubbish. That was, until the tramp came along, wearing old distressed herringbone trousers, waistcoat, odd shoes and socks, fingerless gloves, a simmit (vest), a tartan bow tie (of course), and a red wig and old bowler hat.

This character was a "first" for me, character number two—Barni, shorthand for Barnabas, the encourager. As she started to rake through the rubbish, Barni uncovered a poster advertising what sounded like a very exciting nativity play. As Barni imagined how much fun it would be to go to it, she realized that the date was already past. Forlorn at having missed the opportunity, she still went on rummaging through the bin. All this was in silent mime, with my son Mark playing the flute in the background. The bin yielded many treasures. A discarded wooden box that once held fruit or vegetables, with a little imagination, became a manger, filled with other rubbish and placed on the upturned bin. The hard remains of a partly eaten stale loaf was carefully wrapped in a rag and cradled in Barni's arms—there were no prizes for guessing who this might be, as the loaf "child" was shown to the congregation, and then placed lovingly in the box "manger." Reflecting on that old poster advertising the nativity play (in Kilwinning parish, of course, for this occasion), Barni decided she could have her own, and proceeded to become, in turn, a shepherd dressed in an old blanket taken from the bin, then a king, wearing on her head a crown roughly crafted from a piece of foil that had obviously been used in the cooking of a pre-Christmas meal. After briefly kneeling as each character, she toddled off with a few tangerines, an old coat and other things rescued from the bin that might be enjoyed later in the day—when Barni would be huddled in a shop doorway, and the congregation would all be enjoying a nutritious meal inside their warm homes.

But as she left, something from the discarded poster caught her attention and dragged this tramp back to the bin. The words seemed to leap out with new significance, especially the insistence that this Christmas celebration was for everyone. As Barni looked skyward, pondering on what this might mean, she seemed to receive the amazing affirmation that all this did indeed take place for no less a one than Barni in person.

As the flute continued to play a selection of Christmas music, evoking images of the personal nature of the gift of the Christ-child, Barni returned to the crib with the treasured tangerines, knelt and replaced them, before bowing to pray and then making to walk away. As the music continued, and the connotation of the words of the final carol ("What can I give him, poor as I am . . .?") dawned on her, she took off the shabby coat (one of the more valuable items retrieved from the bin) and placed it across the loaf in the box to provide some additional warmth, before retreating on tiptoe. In the process, Barni turned and saw the child in the pulpit (who had been watching from her "window" all along), returned her cheery wave, and then disappeared. Meanwhile, the child came down quietly and left her own very special and treasured toy at the dustbin manger before going back to be with her dad, who was still engrossed in his paper and hadn't seen a thing.

Not a word had been spoken through this entire "sermon," but there were more than a few damp eyes among those who could have sworn they knew the story backwards.

This then led naturally into the prayers of intercession without any hiatus. How else could you respond?

During the singing of the next carol, the clowns helped the children to bring in their baskets of gifts. These were simple offerings that they had been preparing in advance over a period of several weeks, consisting of fir cones sprayed silver and each with a little tag saying "As a fir cone opens up in the warmth, may you become open to God's love this Christmas." There was one for absolutely everyone, and time was taken until the children had distributed them in an unhurried fashion. I still have my cone and it comes out every year to be included with our own family Christmas decorations. And I still pray for the community who shared that very special service.

But it was not over yet, because as the church choir, who had so ably facilitated this flexible worship, sang the Graham Kendrick song "Peace to You," the clowns brought in another, final box with a large gift tag attached, which simply had the one word "Peace" on it. Out came eight meters of white organza, sparkling as the gold thread running through it was caught in the lights. As the singing continued, they wafted this across the congregation. It was only later when I was watching a video of the service that I saw that people all over the congregation were reaching up to this fabric with their hands, as if to receive and touch the peace of God. And these were Scottish Presbyterians, who are supposed to have a reputation for conservatism. As the final benediction was pronounced and Barni and the minister walked down the aisle together towards the door to greet the congregation, it seemed natural for me to lift my bowler hat and throw it in the air in a final gesture of celebration and blessing. "Even so, come Lord Jesus" took on new meaning in the light of Barni's Christmas.

But even that was not the final amen on this occasion. We all went to the church hall for a Christmas lunch provided and paid for by the choir, who included everyone in their invitation—because, they said, they didn't get the chance to work at helping because they had been too busy practicing singing. It was a beautifully touching gesture.

Authenticity

So that's how Barni came to life. In Scotland we have a saying that "It's better felt than telt"—meaning that it is better to feel it than tell it. This is never more true than with clowning. But I hope this conveys something of the feeling as you let your imagination roam.

As a footnote, let me add that I have always been very concerned that my tramp character should in no way be patronizing to those who are forced to live this way on the margins of society. I felt I had the affirmation of that when I was in Shetland a few years later. By then, Barni had found a voice and on that particular occasion I had done a spoken reflection as I pulled from my backpack various items that I had found while rummaging through the community's dustbins—big nails, half a loaf, a mouthful of wine in a discarded bottle, a coil of barbed wire, and so on. My comments were not intended to be a sermon as such, more in the nature of random observations and throwaway remarks which, for those with ears to hear, related these items to the stories of Jesus. Unbeknown to me, in the congregation that night were two men who had spent much of their lives on the streets as hobos. At the end they made straight for me, and said, "That's exactly what it was like living rough"—and they hugged me. I think, for me, that was Barni's ordination, and though they didn't appreciate it at the time, they were the bishops laying their hands on my head.

Chapter 4

A Clown in the Church

One of the earliest events in my clowning career was in 1988. Throughout the 1980s a major attempt was made to reclaim old dockland and other derelict sites in Britain, and the preferred way of doing this was to create a "garden festival" on these sites. This is probably best described as a cross between a classical garden and a theme park. One such garden festival was proposed for the dockland on Clydeside in Glasgow, which had once supported thriving shipyards but had fallen into disuse with the downturn in demand for large vessels, resulting in the closure of engineering works and a significant increase in the number of people who now found themselves without work. In 1986, captains of Scottish industry and leaders from other walks of life were invited to a promotional presentation by the company that had been commissioned to organize a garden festival in the city of Glasgow. The event was to be held over a six-month period a couple of years later, and the message of the organizers was simple: "If you have a product to promote in 1988, do it at the Glasgow Garden Festival." It so happened that the churches did have "a product to promote" as just a short time before they had agreed to mark 1988 as "Year of the Bible."

Running Fast to Keep Up with God

The Scottish ecumenical group of which John was now convener urged the two of us to go and find out about this garden festival idea, and so a couple of weeks after the formal presentation we found ourselves sitting with the chief executive of the company, asking if at some point in the year a small corner could be made available for the churches to celebrate this particular project. Since the churches had already secured a site for their own pavilion, we had something to work on, but in the context of celebrating "Year of the Bible" the conversation naturally turned to the Bible itself. "Why do you think people would be interested in the Bible anyway?" was the question—in response to which we enthusiastically pointed out its historical importance in our culture, and the continuing significance of its message for today.

The executive evidently got the message—or decided to call our bluff! At any rate, he commented that if the Bible was as important as we were apparently claiming, then a small event in a corner would hardly do it justice. As a result, we were offered the entire 120-acre site for one of the major Christian festivals: Pentecost Sunday. More than that, the company running the garden festival would finance the event. After all, they were paying entertainers on other days throughout the summer season, and to them Pentecost Sunday was just another day.

There was a catch, of course: the Scottish Churches Council would have to produce enough Christian artists and performers with sufficiently varied skills to provide a balanced program throughout the whole site for the entire day. That was quite a challenge, because it amounted to a total of well over 100 program hours. However, not only did it all come to pass, but with an attendance in excess of 47,000 it turned out to be the largest single event to take place throughout the whole of the six months for which the garden festival was open—and in due course the Scottish Churches Council received a gold medal from a government agency to prove it.

I learned a lot from that experience, not least that God is at work in the world—and probably moving well ahead of us—even before we do anything. The apparently unchristian world of Western culture is nothing like as hostile to the gospel as some church people like to think. Why? Because this is God's world, and God is at work in it. The *missio Dei* was not just a concept that theologians talked about, but translated into reality even in this most commercial of undertakings.

So in due course I found myself going down the elevator of a Glasgow hotel on the morning of Sunday, May 22, 1988, dressed as Valentine. It was one of my very earliest appearances, and when a man in a business suit politely asked, "Where are you going?" and my response was "To church," this was clearly much more than he knew how to cope with. It was a bit like the story of the first Pentecost, I thought—they seemed like they must be drunk, but they couldn't really be, could they? (Acts 2:13). And the Valentine outfit would certainly have qualified as a "different language."

Throughout that day I visited all the venues where artists were taking part, to affirm and encourage them. Salvation Army bands wanted their leaders photographed with Valentine, and it was very exciting for me to see not only the warm response to me personally, but also what was possible when the resources of creative talent of the Scottish churches were brought together in one place. That achievement alone proved to be a significant affirmation for many creative people who had often struggled with knowing how they might use their skills in the service of the Church. But I was equally if not more encouraged by the openness of many of the artists who were on the permanent staff at the garden festival, who embraced me as one of their own, and engaged with me in conversation about what I was doing and how the public were receiving me. Telling why I was there gave me a new insight into what sharing my faith in the real world could mean. There was no need for me to preach: all I had to do was to give an account of myself. As well as being enormous fun, I reflected later that it was also a very biblical way of being (see 1 Peter 3:15).

Each event Valentine attended seemed to lead to another invitation. I found myself being asked to many different venues, including schools and prisons. I always make a point of trying to have advance conversations with the leaders of any group I am going to work with. Even if church leaders have been understandably wary in advance, when they see that I am not just interested in doing a "show" but genuinely want to integrate what I do with their own work, the dynamic usually changes. I have to remember that I am probably not the first clown they have met, and that their previous experiences might easily have been very negative ones from some different source. As a child, they could have been frightened by a clown or other character whom they will then unconsciously associate with me. This is where Christian integrity is supremely important. As a Christian clown, I take Jesus as my model, which means that I need to do what Jesus did—and he always affirmed people and lifted them up. People who met Jesus always went away feeling better: he had the knack of valuing people, helping them to feel good about themselves—and yet at the same time moving them on and challenging them. This balance between affirmation and challenge is something we have largely lost, but I believe that clowning can be a significant way of rediscovering how to do it.

In schools, I usually try to link into whatever special themes the children might be working on in their regular curriculum. I remember visiting Lundin Links Primary School in Fife, at the invitation of the Church of Scotland field-worker who was their chaplain. I talked with the head teacher in advance and then to each teacher in turn, with the result that each class was able to integrate some aspect of clowning into their ordinary work. So, for instance, tiny ones (four- and five-year-olds) worked using shapes to make clown faces. Another class made biscuits, again using shapes. An older class did a classic clown sketch using a huge newspaper—but the facts they discovered were related to research on a project to help them understand AIDS and the associated risks to themselves. Yet another class worked on classic mime skills to create human machines, which was a project in collaboration and team-building. The superstars of the sports field and gym hall did cartwheels and somersaults. The senior class dressed the younger ones as clowns as part of a project in health, well-being and caring. Even mathematics was included, as older students tried to work out the parabola traced by a clown's juggling clubs!

This kind of thing went on all term, and then when the special day came the clowns visited the school. I was greeted by the music teacher who said, "It's wonderful: I have just come from the paper shop and the whole conversation in the town is about what's happening in school today." The children arrived in clown costumes for the day and a number of parents came in specially to help, including one dad who made a video of the whole event. We met in the hall, which was circular and had been decorated to make it look like a circus big top. The children's artwork was displayed around the wall, pictures of themselves sitting together as if on the edge of the circle at a circus arena, while their handmade puppets hung from the ceiling like acrobats. The whole school came in and I told the story of Valentine and got dressed up (similarly to the way I described in chapter 1). After that, the clowns visited each classroom. It was especially good to have enough helpers with me so that every class could have their very own clown. They also took turns going into the circus tent (school hall) and learning to juggle and spin plates and do traditional clown things.

During that time, one little boy came and sought me out and asked, "Was that a true story about Valentine?" I assured him that it was. "But the baby didn't really die, did she?" As I spent time chatting with him, I discovered that the child had been through a painful family experience and it was important for him to know that Valentine's story was true and that she had been able to carry on and find healing and help.

When lunchtime arrived, we went to the canteen and all the cooks and servers were wearing their own red noses and had created a menu with clown names for every item. The whole place had entered into the spirit of things. After lunch, there was a great busyness to get everyone ready for the grand finale. On the stroke of two o'clock, the piano imitated a drum roll and each class marched in. In turn they presented their own clown sketches, just as if they were in a real circus. It was a wonderful day, and I received a letter later from the head teacher saying, "We thought about asking you back to repeat this for our Easter service, but then we realized the children could actually do it themselves and tell the Easter story through this medium." I could have thought of no more effective outcome: they hadn't just seen a show, they had become part of the story, and the story had become part of them. Some real facilitation and empowerment had taken place.

After that, I had invitations from other schools in the area, who had read about the event and wanted to explore its possibilities for themselves. One head said, "Our school is going through refurbishment and it's an awful mess, everyone's fed up and the teachers are so depressed. Can you come and give us a lift?"

Schools are not the only institutions in our community. I suppose the opposite end to school is prison, though some children feel they are the same thing. But how could clowning be any use in prison? Well, I have been to many prisons now—from women's jails to young offenders' institutions, and have met inmates right across the spectrum, from people serving life sentences to those preparing for release. The gospel translates into every situation. It is just a matter of working to make relevant connections. I have found that mime is one of the most useful techniques to use in a prison. It is so open ended that it leaves space to enter the action from whatever point people find they are at. Perhaps this is more important here than in other circumstances, because prisoners have so few real choices that they are able to make for themselves.

As I was planning a visit to one men's prison and thinking of what I might do, I reckoned it would be fairly predictable that I would face some particular heckling due to the fact that I was a woman. I have a sketch about my heart, which I take out and play with. I describe it in more detail in appendix 2. In the process, I drop the heart and it breaks into pieces before God eventually intervenes and mends it. This sketch is versatile because I can do it when I work alone. But it works better if I have another clown to work with, as I can throw my heart to my partner a few times, and then, when they have the idea of what to do, I usually throw it to a member of the audience. It occurred to me in advance of the event that if I did this in a prison, I could probably expect at least one of the inmates to keep it and pretend to run off with it. To be forewarned is to be forearmed—because that is exactly what did happen. I could have berated him (in mime of course), chased him to retrieve it, or given him a hard time in some other way, but I knew that would make little or no impact because he had to deal with that sort of thing every day. So I just became dejected. Instead of trying to regain control, I became the vulnerable one (which is what the sketch is all about anyway). The prisoner could literally have done whatever he liked with my heart—jumped on it, broken it, whatever. As it was, in due course he returned and threw it back to me. As I caught it, we laughed at each other, and then I continued with the sketch as planned. It was a very special moment. I don't know how God spoke to that man through that episode, but I'm happy to leave it there. God will have done a much more complete job than I could, being able to stay with him long after I'd gone home.

I used the same sketch in a church in Teesside, England, and a teenager jumped up and "headed" the heart back as if we were playing a football match. Brilliant! On the streets of Berkeley, California, some Japanese children who could speak absolutely no English, and with whom therefore I could never have communicated in words, caught my heart and threw it back, much to their parents' delight—a response which let me know that they understood what was going on, even though they had no English either.

After doing this sketch at a training event at Fuller Seminary for church workers, a Hispanic American family from downtown Los Angeles approached me. Only the mother could speak English, while Dad and their 14-year-old daughter just grinned. But Mom explained that they had come from Mexico to work among poor immigrant workers in an outreach from the Roman Catholic cathedral, and that her daughter had absolutely loved that sketch and would like to be able to share it in the ghetto. I could never have spoken with these people myself, but I was deeply honored to know that I had an appropriate gift that would be of some use to them. "Please take it," I said. "Use it." I would love to see how it developed in that context. It is just one sketch—but it has had so many responses.

Affirmation from the Churches

Church leaders became very interested in what I was doing. Almost at the end of my "Arabian" experience, which I referred to in the first chapter, I had a call from a local minister. He floated the idea of me taking a service in his church during Holy Week. I was very excited because up to that point I had not taken a service as a clown. The thing that encouraged me was that, without any prompting, he had personally made the connection between the Holy Fool and Jesus, and so I eagerly agreed to go although it felt a bit scary. It was a Church of Scotland congregation in a very deprived area where there was no tradition of regularly going to church, and the Christians had to work hard at making connections with others in the community. As I look back, I realize now that these people were certainly God's instrument in leading me on to a new stage in this journey. I am particularly glad that it should have been so, because clowns have real empathy with the poor and marginalized—and through that, continuity with Jesus.

Since then, I have been regularly inundated with invitations to take services. One of the most interesting—and exciting—aspects of this ministry is that the places to which I am most often asked to go are not grand or trendy churches. They are very ordinary, filled with ordinary people who are probably struggling to discover how to "be church" in their particular community. Mostly—and certainly on my first visit—I go dressed in my ordinary clothes, tell my story, and in the process transform myself into Valentine. Like many of the best stories, I always keep it simple. In particular, the central theme is always the point when I come to have the crosses painted on my eyes, and I am invited to begin to see the world the way God sees it, through the cross. This, I think, is the reason why many clergy have been so affirming of what I do. They see that, far from being a gimmick, this is an affirmation of the essentials of the Christian faith which has continuity with all mainline Christian traditions and is simply a creative way of expressing what they feel their life's work is about. I find it especially encouraging that this is the case right across the traditions. No one denomination holds all the truth, and the work of evangelization requires us to work together and learn from one another to fulfill the apostolic task of sharing the gospel with the people of the world.

Whatever else may be said about it, Christian clowning as I am interpreting it is certainly not weak on theology: in fact, I find that the more theologically informed people are, the more likely they are to make the connections without me having to spell it out for them.

I remember having lunch with about a dozen prominent Christian leaders in the exhibitors' restaurant in the Scottish Exhibition and Conference Center (SECC) in Glasgow. Lunch was hosted by Gospatric Home, Director of the Christian Resources Exhibition (CRE), for his honored guests and I found myself sitting next to Bishop Mario Conti, Roman Catholic bishop of Aberdeen—he was in his fancy dress, and I in mine! Without any explanation from me, he made the immediate connection with the crosses on my eyes. I will always remember the look of wonder on his face as he said, "It's about vulnerability, isn't it?"

We continued talking over lunch, but one thing that a clown cannot ignore when in costume is other people. I became aware of growing excitement at a nearby table, where three children were sitting having lunch with their parents and obviously commenting about me. To have integrity with my clown character, I had to give a discreet wave. Soon we were having an animated conversation at a distance, using hand signals, and in due course I excused myself from where I was sitting and went over and introduced myself to them. Their parents were working at an ice-cream exhibition that was taking place in the same venue. We all talked about what we were doing there and they told me they lived in Aberdeen, and then, probably because they could see that my security badge said "Christian Resources Exhibition," they told me they were Christians of the Roman Catholic tradition. Well, what else could I say except, "There's someone you will want to meet: I'm having lunch with your bishop." With great delight, he came over and as I left them they were all having a very positive pastoral encounter. Valentine was simply the catalyst, doing what Christian clowns have always done: drawing attention to One greater than themselves (the One who is greater even than their bishops).

One church in the west of Scotland invited me to go and lead what they described as their "awayday at home"—if you can work that out. There were all sorts of exciting things to do, including a bouncy castle for the kids throughout the day. It's a parish where I have now led several days of this kind, so as I look back, the various events tend to merge with one another in my memory. On one occasion I clowned with them in the morning, and then after lunch for "a bit of a rest" we had some songs. During the half hour's singing (with me dressed as Valentine), a little girl had squeezed her seat up to sit next to me. I think she could only have been about four years old. I was very aware that she kept gazing up into my face, and I knew I was under deep scrutiny. I smiled once or twice but really didn't want to distract people from their thoughts, so I just acted "normal." I don't know who chose the song "God forgave my sin in Jesus' name," but when it was chosen I knew I wanted to share with them a dance to the song that I had previously done in my own church with a child. So I whispered to the child next to me, "Would you like to help me?" The response was immediate, and her vigorous head-nodding suggested that this was just what she had been waiting for. "Well," I said, "you just copy me."

It only involved her mirroring my actions, but in order to be at her height I had to kneel. As we were doing it, I knew that I was enjoying myself, and I found it most moving to see this child's trusting response as she followed me in something she had never done in her life before. But I was unprepared for what came next, for as we got to the end and we looked up at those around us, almost every single person had tears streaming down their faces. Was it the vulnerability of the child, or the clown, or just the fact that the person leading that particular session had for a moment relinquished control? Even now, several years later, when I occasionally meet anyone from this church, I can guarantee that at some point in conversation they will say, "I remember when the little girl . . ." Would that all our ministry had that sort of lasting impact, not just in terms of memorable pictures in our minds, but as change in our lives.

On another occasion with the same group, I made masks and at the end of the day we used them in worship. While standing quietly behind the cross as people were making their responses, I felt enormously privileged to see an older woman, who I think was the grandmother of the family, go and take hold of a couple with three children, one of whom was seriously disabled, and they all came forward together, hand in hand, and laid their masks at the foot of the cross. I don't know the details of what was going on, only that it was evident that God was at work.

One of the things I like most about clowning is that there is always room to learn. Though it sounds both stupid and unlikely, since childhood I have been paranoid about "making a fool of myself." In my imagination, I can still hear my mother asking, "Whatever will people think?" I have worked several times at Christian Resources Exhibitions around the UNITED KING-DOM, and they always present me with learning opportunities. The one in question was in Glasgow and the organizers had issued a big media invitation to radio, TV, newspaper reporters, and everybody who was deemed to be anybody. Valentine and the dancers mentioned in Chapter 2 were doing a mini-presentation in the central thoroughfare in front of a dais full of celebrities and surrounded by very expensive state-of-the-art PA equipment. Space was a bit limited and, of course, as Valentine enthusiastically threw herself into the action her size 18 shoes collided with the amplifiers and the noise ricocheted around that barn of a place. Olive would have been mortified at her stupidity, but Valentine merely reacted as though the speaker had shouted at her, and turned to a shrivelling jelly, much to everyone's amusement. They thought it had all been intentional—but now they know! Being Valentine has taught me that it's okay to make mistakes—something that is personally very liberating indeed.

One of the most treasured photos in my scrapbook is a cutting from the front page of *The Scotsman* newspaper, and shows me sitting in the Assembly Hall of the Church of Scotland at the Annual Meeting of the Women's Guild in 1993. I had been asked to condense my story into a very limited and very precise time-frame—twelve and a half minutes. Considering that I can easily take up to forty minutes with a clown sermon, that would have been no small feat at any time. But right then, I had been going through a very anxious period in my life and I really didn't think I had what it took to go and do this. I remember telling God from my knees, "You've got me into all this, so you really are going to have to pull it together, as I simply haven't got what it takes." This is obviously what I should do all the time, because I still meet surprising numbers of people who say to me, years later, "I was at the Guild." That phrase has become a shorthand expression for all that happened that day—almost, it seems, in the way that people remember where they were when Princess Diana died, or Kennedy was shot.

The fact that my presentation made such a huge impact also shows that it's not the number of words that count. I remember being relieved when I got there to discover that I was provided with a radio mike, which meant that I would be able to move. At one point I turned round and found myself face to face with the Moderator of the General Assembly of the Church of Scotland, who was sitting only a few feet away but in an elevated position at about my head height. Naturally, he was wearing the traditional attire of Moderators of the General Assembly, which at that time included tight black leggings together with shoes with big shiny buckles and a black coat with fancy silver buttons and lots of bits of white lace. As I told the story of Valentine and put my clown coat on (which also was covered with silver sequins and fancy bits and bobs), I spontaneously took one look at him and surprised even myself as I said, "I'm obviously not the only one with a funny coat." Fortunately for me, he had the good grace to laugh heartily and the whole company erupted. It was truly a God-given moment. But as a result of that occasion I have subsequently shared my story with thousands of women throughout the length and breadth of Scotland. Sometimes they have flocked to meet me in their hundreds, at other times I have been with only a handful in some remote rural parish. On many occasions I have been privileged to pray with them or hear of their own journeys of faith through difficult times, but whoever they have been, every one of them has enriched my life.

After sharing my story so often, I have sometimes found myself asking, "Am I doing this automatically? Is this losing its sparkle? Sometimes this is just too painful and I'd like not to go on. Am I making things worse for myself?" Yet every time I have entertained such misgivings, someone has come and told me how the story has touched and helped them. I have now come to realize that it will be time to stop only when the story ceases to touch people's lives—but until then I am called to go on.

Encouraging Others

After a time, some people began to ask me, "How can I get started in this Christian clowning?" So I decided to hold my first workshop. It was low-key and held just at my local church in Stirling, but it was a great start and we had lots of fun. My husband, John, was lifting, carrying, and generally being helpful. I discovered later that a young woman had hitched a lift from Aberdeen, a distance of about 120 miles. She had previously trained as a clown at circus school, but she had seen an advertisement somewhere for this workshop on Christian clowning and so she came to see what it was all about. She had been living with a New Age community, whose leader had decided that they should read the Bible as part of their spiritual growth. So they did, and as she read it, Angela found herself attracted by what she read, and in due course she committed herself to what she knew about this Jesus person she had been reading about, left the New Age group—and only a short time later landed in my workshop. John was interested in both the New Age and the Bible, but even he was taken aback when she produced a Bible from her bag, asked him if he knew anything about it, and proceeded to quiz him on the identity of the many thousands of people listed in the book of Numbers. Her fascination with them was engendered by the fact that they represented a long line of spiritual understanding, passed on from one generation to another —something that Angela found really attractive about the Bible, for she wanted to be a part of that sort of unbroken tradition of faith. I don't think she ever did get an answer to her question, but she has since gone on to become a very accomplished storyteller and is now working full-time in assisting the churches in Britain in finding new ways of telling the gospel story to our communities.

Some time later, I organized a training day at Stirling University and Roly Bain—an Anglican priest who at that time had just moved into full-time clown ministry—came and worked with me. At the end of the day I threw out an invitation to any who wanted to take it forward to leave their names on a list. The stimulus for this was that Action of Churches Together in Scotland (ACTS) was planning a national ecumenical celebration, and I had been invited to contribute some kind of clown presentation. From that list developed a group who came to be known as "Celtic Christian Clowns," which now functions as a loose network of Christian clowns who come together particularly (though not exclusively) for national Scottish events, especially ecumenical ones. The group includes people from the Church of Scotland, as well as Methodists, Baptists, Episcopalians, and Pentecostals—in other words, though the denominational spread could be even more comprehensive, they represent a broad spectrum of the Church in Scotland. We have done a number of events, including an hour-long theater production for Advent 1998 under the auspices of ACTS in the Scottish Exhibition and Conference Center. We usually don't go for a written script—we are all much too adventurous for that. We take the long and treacherous route of working something out together, which means we can use the talents we might each have at any given time, rather than starting with a preconceived idea of what we want and inevitably either trying to fit square pegs into round holes or excluding someone. It takes time to work like this but the end result is usually very rewarding. Everyone is able to contribute, and thereby they can own both the process and the outcome.

If I remember rightly, the youngest member of this group, Kate, must only have been about nine when we first came together, and the way in which the others accepted her and took account of her opinions and ideas at each stage is itself an interesting comment on the potential that clowning has for helping to create a genuinely intergenerational sense of community.

I'll return to Kate's distinctive contribution later in the chapter, but looking even further back, I suppose the initial stirrings that led to the formation of this group can probably be traced to an invitation I got from a church in Fife. The minister asked me to have workshops with her young people one Saturday and prepare something that could then be used in the Sunday services the next day. Being a small rural parish, the church had a beautiful hall that had formerly been stables, and an orchard outside. It was the first weekend the youngsters had gone back to school after the long summer holidays, and the weather was fine and sunny. We juggled inside and out, and had great fun. The minister's husband was very helpful, willing to make numerous snacks and refreshments, but he issued a stern warning to me right at the beginning: "I'll do anything to help, but don't give me a red nose." So I didn't.

I did, however, discover that he was already a very skilled juggler. I remember thinking to myself what a wasted talent that could be if he was not also a clown—but I knew I had to leave him space to be himself. Jesus always offers us the opportunity, but leaves us free to make our own choices—which I thought was a pity, because I would dearly have loved to twist his arm.

However, when I returned on the Sunday morning, who had a red nose on? Exactly. And who led the procession into church, juggling clubs and accompanied by the congregation singing "I will enter God's gates with thanksgiving in my heart"—all the while being filmed by a crew from an international TV network? Dave (for that is his name), and his long-standing buddy, Doug.

That wasn't the only challenge of that particular weekend. The film crew told my roadie (my husband John again) that they knew the woman in the culottes with the guitar was the minister, but they just couldn't get it into their heads, and kept wanting to get permission to do things from the assistant minister, who happened to be a man wearing a dog collar, and who therefore fitted their image more easily.

But back to Dave and Doug, for today they are two of the best clowns I know in Scotland. One is an Auguste clown, the other a white-face, and since that time they have kept working and improving their skills, which are mostly based around slapstick routines. They are part of the Celtic Christian Clowns group, but do a lot of work on their own and have proved to be a great asset to many young people's groups and churches in Scotland. I could never do the slapstick stuff. People often remark with surprise that they find me to be a very gentle clown, I think perhaps because they don't often meet gentle clowns. But both my characters are quite deliberately understated.

Clownbo (Tommy Thomson) is another of the Celtic Christian Clowns—a "professor of balloonology," as he likes to be known. He can make absolutely anything out of balloons—and talk at the same time. He is at his best on the streets, and his non-stop patter engages the people of his native Glasgow in a particularly effective way. It was only years later that we worked out that he also had attended the weekend course in Leith, led by Philip Noble, that launched me into clowning.

Jangle is the jester clown referred to in chapter 3. She didn't become a clown until into her fifties. She was already one of my best friends, which is one reason why I never invited or encouraged her to join me in this enterprise. I never actually discouraged her either, because I had a feeling that, as she journeyed with God for herself, this might easily be a direction she would eventually take. But I knew it would have to be her own thing, and resisted the temptation to articulate what she wanted to say as she worked at clarifying her own spiritual path. It was the right approach. God had been challenging her, but she needed to make her own decision, so that when she came on board it was with much greater commitment. The way she chose her clown name sums up much of her story. She had heard the story of Michelangelo working with hammer and chisel on a block of stone and explaining what he was doing by saying, "I"m releasing the angel imprisoned inside this block of stone." "That's it," she thought, "that's what God wants to do with me." Being a lover of crosswords, she juggled with the letters and thought, "Mmm . . . angel . . . rearrange it and you get angle . . . add J for Jesus and you get . . . Jangle: Jesus has the best angle on things." And so Jangle the Jester came to birth.

Heather is another one who became a clown in her fifties. I remember that because she got my phone number from someone else and then called me and asked, "Am I too old to start?" She had great trouble finding who her clown might be until she discovered the fabric she liked for her clothes. But when she identified her character Bluebell, things developed very fast indeed as she brought her life's experience to the situation. She too became an effective storyteller and an expert at spinning plates. As I've gotten to know more clowns around the world, I've noticed that there are many midlife to older people among them, including some into their seventies and eighties. I wonder if age gives people greater freedom to be themselves?

Then there are Andy and Diane, a younger couple with boundless energy who announced to the assembled company of Celtic Christian Clowns one day that there was to be a new clown, who turned out to be their firstborn, Lucy. Since then, Peter has also joined them and us. They will travel endlessly to support the group, and their baby carriage decorated with streamers and balloons is a sight to behold. We are a growing family!

Joyce was a lay staff worker for the Church of Scotland who, on her own admission, had always had a clumsy streak—but it wasn't until she acknowledged this and allowed her natural style to work for her that she discovered all sorts of routines that could be a real advantage to a clown.

Daz, the six-footer in bright red-and-white striped Cossack-style trousers, black tailcoat and royal blue bowler decorated with a sunflower, is my son Andrew, whom you met as a five-year-old in the first chapter. It was a particular joy to me that he chose to be involved in clown ministry—though no surprise, as even when he was small he would regularly come from school highly delighted when the class had fallen about laughing at his antics. Daz's significant gift became the bestowing of blessings, one of his favorite tricks being to cross himself, uttering the words "Lux—Omo—Domestos—Brut," which I have a feeling is almost too obvious in print, but when spoken has an authentic Latin sound about it. It usually takes people a minute to realize what is going on before they fall about laughing—and then the "real" blessing can come in.

Alison was a schoolteacher who had a really hard time in her church, as a result of which her faith was tested. Clowning brought her a release to discover new horizons and apply her considerable experience as a primary school teacher to solving many a sticky problem for us.

Space becomes a problem when I start to think of the others who have joined us from time to time—but I recall with affection Joanne, Kentigern, Gordon, Alisdair, Claire, Linda, Mark, Alethea, Neil, Dawn, Graeme, Margaret and Ian, all of whom have contributed different skills and talents into this ministry at various points in time over the last ten years or so.

Memorable Occasions

This group has become simply a network of Christian clowns supporting one another. We only come together for special events. When I am personally invited to major events, I usually ask others to opt in as their diaries allow. This allows a safe place for new people to explore their talents. New members will generally have been to at least one workshop before they would join in. The result of working together and supporting each other has now made available to the wider church the resources of groups and individual clowns based across Scotland who can be involved at many levels of evangelism and worship. This has been particularly useful in parishes that may be trying to bridge the gap between church and community at events like community fairs.

I have been especially encouraged by some of the national events I have been invited to, not least because the organizers see our work as continuous with and complementary to theirs. For several years we supported the annual carol concert in the Usher Hall in Edinburgh, a major fund-raising event for the hospital in Nazareth operated by the Edinburgh Medical Missionary Society. Handshaking with those waiting to get in, sometimes in the snow, dusting them down, tapping them on the shoulder and seeing the surprise when they turn round, greeting people as they arrive in taxis and buses, sweeping the way in front of a person in a wheelchair and seeing the crowd step aside while the person in the wheelchair becomes the celebrity is nothing short of a delight. Inevitably we also engage with people out on the street who are just going about their business, and bring a little joy to them.

The Royal Hospital for Sick Children in Edinburgh had a whole year of special fund-raising as part of their centenary celebrations, and at the culmination of their efforts they invited all the children who had been treated, and their schools and teachers, to attend a big service of thanksgiving, again held in the Church of Scotland's Assembly Hall on the Mound. This is an easily recognizable site to all tourists to Edinburgh's Princes Street, as it is the only building with twin spires on the skyline below the castle, and in recent times it has been the temporary home of the Scottish Parliament. The place was packed. The anchor person was Steve Fischbacher, a songwriter gifted in work with primary school children whose wife had been a member of a Bible class I had been teaching in Stirling at the time my daughter died. His music is loved by children and adults alike, not least because—like my clowning—it has emerged out of the joys and pain of his own life experience. His young wife Lynda died, and Steve's ministry has been dominated by the struggle of coming to terms with her loss and finding himself as a lone parent of two small children.

The buzz of hundreds of children arriving in bus loads, and the expectant wonder in their eyes, just brings out the best in clowns. Greeting takes on a new form. Maybe the welcomers at our church doors should try it. Just before the event was about to start, Daz entered in his tailcoat and, with feather duster in hand, invited everyone to stand (no words). Everyone did. He walked away, but they stayed standing—until he came back and motioned them to sit down again. The scene was set for fun and laughter.

Among other things that happened that day, we opened up our huge yellow Bible for the reading and blew the dust away, while Jangle and Valentine had particular fun with the heart sketch that I've already described—it seemed to fit in perfectly for a hospital event. Jangle's dentist husband had been persuaded to design all sorts of imaginative medical-looking instruments that squeaked and squirted. A central feature of this particular hall is a kind of enclosed dais with rails all round it, affectionately known as "the pen" because it looks a bit like a place where you might keep animals. We had great fun tumbling over the pen rails to take the pulses of hospital managers and medics, to hoots of laughter from the children. We helped the choirs of children to relax, and their conductors and pianists too—dusting them well and winding them up as if they were clockwork! It's amazing how much better people sing when they are smiling. It was a real celebration, and we were overjoyed at the response from the hospital's chief nursing officer, who said she wished the church could be like that. So did we.

An invitation to Christian Aid's Scottish Celebration of its fiftieth anniversary in the historic Church of the Holy Rude at Stirling was another real whoopee of an occasion. As a resident of Stirling, I knew only too well the history of this somewhat dark and austere building, which at one stage of its recent history had had a wall built right down the middle so that two warring factions could worship in the same building without having to meet! In most churches, the east end is likely to be slightly higher than the rest, but in this church it is actually lower, almost like a shallow pit, which is wonderful for an orchestral concert but presented major difficulties for anything of a dramatic nature. A clown brain helps to get around this.

We decided to tell the story of the great feast (Luke 14:14-23) and contextualize it by having the king's servant go out into the somewhat deprived area around the church and invite the drug addicts, the single parents, and those sleeping in the shop doorways to come to the feast. Most events never quite run to plan, and this one was no exception. The night before, my lead clown for the day (Dave, the one who was never going to wear a red nose) phoned to say that his wife was about to give birth to their first child, and not surprisingly he was unable to attend the feast. The story as Jesus told it was already starting to seem all too real. So on the morning of the event, I rewrote the script, arrived at the church on our agreed schedule and greeted the team with the good news that Dave was about to become a father, but what I thought would be the bad news that we would have to start again from the beginning. As I explained how I thought we could rearrange things, Kate (who was just twelve) listened, took it all in, and subsequently performed absolutely brilliantly as the king. In fact, by common consent, she was the star of the event. Only afterwards did I realize that I had made absolutely no concessions to her age, but it didn't matter for she had always been accepted in the group and her opinion valued, so that when the opportunity came, it all easily translated into responsibility and growth for her.

There was just one problem: because she wasn't tall enough to be easily visible from the lower level of floor at the front of the church, I needed to get something for her to stand on behind the banqueting table, to play her part as the king. I tentatively asked the beadle if there would be something she might stand on, and he indicated a chair standing in the corner. Even I could see that this was no ordinary chair: it was made of dark wood with a very high carved back, a big flat seat and huge arms. To get my point across, and ensure that I would not find myself in trouble later on, I said quite pointedly, "But Kate needs to stand on it . . . she might even stamp her foot on it"—to which the reply was, "Well, James VI was one of the last people to sit in it, so it should be strong enough." So Kate stood in the place of the monarchs of Scotland, dressed in her clown gear with the addition of a gold crown, while I read our totally revised and unrehearsed version of the story of the great feast. The great trestle table was covered with enormous cloths, and with the kind of pulling and heaving that only clowns could manage, fruit arrived on spinning plates, goblets were placed on the table having been juggled first, diablos also became containers for wine, but of course the excuses for not attending were fast and furious from all over: gone to do a deal on a new car; just won a time-share holiday; but it's the Cup final . . . the rugby international; might come later; need to check my lottery numbers. Like the king in Jesus's story, Kate got really angry and did indeed stamp her foot on James VI's seat in the unself-conscious way that only a child could, while her crown (which had been designed to fit Dave's rather larger head) fell down over her eyes and ears. But I think those who were there got the message.

In the final response at the end of the celebration, people had been invited to write on slips of paper what they would like to see accomplished in the next stage of Christian Aid's work, including their own personal aims. We had offered our big (about a meter across) brightly colored offering plate to be used for this. Because of circumstances, very little of what we did had been rehearsed, though it had been carefully planned and prayed over. But all of us who were taking part knew that we were not there just to entertain, and the challenge was to us too. So, like everyone else, we wrote our personal responses and prayers and, with that invisible communication through eye and gesture which is a natural part of clowning, we spontaneously decided that we would wait until everyone else had placed their responses in the plate before we would then slowly go forward, kneel down, and add our own.

This reminds me very much of Philemon, a fourth-century clown who worked in the courts of the Roman emperor Diocletian. The emperor had passed a decree that everyone should worship him. Philemon, dressed as a clown, refused, and this was considered a huge joke. The very idea that anyone would disobey the emperor was too preposterous for words. But part of the jester's job is also to challenge the status quo, to invite us to take a close look at ourselves, our motives and intentions. Though Philemon's refusal to worship as a clown evoked hilarity, the emperor was determined that Philemon the person could not be allowed to disobey in this manner, and when he refused to pay homage because of his higher allegiance to God he was executed and became one of the Christian martyrs. Like most Christians today, I am glad my commitment has not been put to that test, whether as clown or person—nor have most Christians in my country at this present time, though historically this has not always been the case, and in other parts of the world people are still persecuted today for their faith. I am, however, glad to be continuous with the model of faith embodied in people like Philemon, and those who are tempted to think of clowning as a gimmick should reflect on his example.

The clown's privileged position of acting as Holy Fool, inviting others to stand back and take a look at themselves from God's perspective, is of course what got the medieval clowns into trouble and ultimately led to them being banished from the Church. But the Holy Fool had a valuable ministerial role in highlighting spiritual and personal folly in a pretentious and exaggerated way that allowed people the opportunity to laugh at themselves. Most of us are more likely to change if we can laugh at ourselves, rather than just having a finger wagged at us. On April 1, All Fools' Day, there was a sort of amnesty for clowns in the medieval Church. It was an occasion for banqueting and celebration, and a day when the fools were allowed to take a rise out of their betters and elders. Sadly, those in authority eventually found it too threatening, and the custom was discontinued and the fools banished. As a result, the Church lost the valuable role of that person calling us to be accountable. The reemergence of the fool in more recent times can help us as Christians to laugh at ourselves again, and to see ourselves as the world sees us.

I am encouraged that many of the church leaders who have affirmed my work most warmly have been bishops and others in similar positions—not that I necessarily regard what they say as more valuable than the insights of others, but I see hope and new possibilities for the Church when such people desire to be challenged in their own styles of ministry and leadership.

Shaking the Foundations

When I am asked to clown in the community, people usually come with simple requests. They ask me what I do, and if they like the sound of it, they invite me to do it for them, and quite often with them. But invitations from religious groups can be more complicated, not least because the control factor frequently comes into play and people feel they need to know exactly what might happen, long before the event.

I had a striking example of this when I was invited to take part in a conference on urban mission. It was part of a regular series of conferences, bringing together people from all walks of life to meet over several days to support one another and explore new ways of sharing the gospel in situations of urban deprivation. A key element in such an event is obviously a whole range of workshops giving participants the opportunity to explore new things. I was asked to lead some workshops on clown ministry, but more particularly also to take part in the final service of dedication and commitment. The organizing committee knew of my Barni character and had heard of a sketch that I have called Barni's Feast. In this, Barni sorts through her bag, pulling out the various treasures that have been rescued from dustbins and the street. Included in this collection will be the items I have already mentioned in describing this character—stale bread, the remains of a bottle of wine, barbed wire, nails, a few cloths, the end of a candle, and other assorted odds and ends. In mime, I set all these things up as a kind of mini-altar, and often invite others to share the bread and wine if they wish.

The relevance of all this to urban deprivation and mission was obvious to the organizing committee, which is why they asked me to do it. But they had a very particular request: would I please just leave the bread and wine on display, have some myself, but not invite others to join in. I talked about it with the chairperson but their position was set in stone. If I'm honest, I would have to admit that I really wasn't too happy about this, but the organizers felt that since it was an ecumenical event, inviting others to share Barni's feast might cause a few problems. For a whole variety of reasons, I was troubled by their failure to be prepared to push the boundaries out. For myself, I felt I had learned so much from the oppressed and marginalized that this was just another form of bourgeois culture trying to control those whose faces don't fit. I also reflected on all the words that have been spoken and written over the years about seeing Christ in the faces of the poor, poverty as a sacrament and so on—sentiments that were, of course, repeated many times during that entire weekend.

But I also knew that at the heart of Christian clowning is weakness and vulnerability. I did not feel that a war of words—not even of good theology!—was the medium of the message I wished to share. In any case, I also felt that I could only do so much and I shouldn't therefore be unwilling to participate just because of the restrictions that were being imposed. So I approached that worship with the same attitude as I take to all these things, trusting that my participation would be led by the Spirit and accomplish whatever God might want at that particular moment. I did exactly as the committee had decreed, leaving the loaf and the bottle on the communion table at the front of the church and retracing my steps as I had arrived—Barni with a sweeping brush, one of the outcasts of society, collecting up anything that looked as if it might be useful.

As I disappeared, I could hardly believe what then happened, for one of the office-bearers of the organizing group (actually, the one with whom I had had the most direct discussion about all this beforehand) jumped up from his seat in the congregation and headed for the front. It was probably just as well for me that by now I had disappeared and could hear what was going on only from a distance: had I seen him jump up, I could have been really worried that, in spite of all the careful planning, I had inadvertently been offensive. But he announced to everyone that, for himself, he was not prepared to leave until he'd shared in Barni's Feast. So Barni was sent for, and brought back into the auditorium, dazed and surprised. By now, there was no stopping the assembled crowd, as people got up out of their seats and pressed forward to be a part of the sharing of the bread and wine. Denominational barriers evaporated and the resultant experience was certainly divine.

As I reflected on it later, it occurred to me that because this was all in silent mime (apart from a musical backing), there was never any chance that it would break any taboos anyway, because the central things that people disagree on in relation to the Eucharist are all connected with words—what the words are, and who says them. It was even more ironic for me to realize that, had I planned to invite this sharing from the outset, I would have included in my bag a beer mug that I normally use for such a purpose, but because of the situation, and thinking that I was the only one who would eat or drink, I left that out and took a swig directly from the wine bottle (which of course is more in tune with what a hobo would be doing anyway). And so there we all were—a hundred or more church leaders sharing a broken crust and a discarded bottle of wine.

Not only for me, but for many others, this seemed to become a living parable of much that had been discussed during that conference. Yet like most parables it also raised a very pointed challenge, which the worship leader then effectively highlighted. Many good and radical things had been said over the preceding days—things that were faithful to the gospel and sensitive to the needs of the urban poor. But to make any headway, we need to act as well as talk. The gospel calls people to change, and that change must begin with those who issue the call—ourselves.

At the lunch following that worship experience, one clergyman whom I have known well for many years and who has consistently been a risk-taking groundbreaker in terms of urban mission, distinctly avoided me even down to refusing any eye contact. I was troubled that he, of all people, should have found this a difficult experience. Several months later, he told me it wasn't that he didn't like it: he simply could not have spoken because he had been so profoundly moved that he would just have wept. Maybe more of us will need to be prepared to shed some tears if we are to see things changed.

Chapter 5

Expanding My Horizons

Beginning with England . . .

Encounters across the border started to occur. One of my earliest memories of these forays was a weekend spent in the village of Faringdon near Oxford. John and I were there together, leading a weekend for the Oxfordshire Baptist Association, as part of which I was invited to be guest preacher at one of an ongoing series of regular ecumenical all-age services. On this occasion, the Sunday morning service was to be held in the Anglican parish church. The church was crowded and had the delightful addition of huge pillars about twelve feet in diameter. In the normal course of affairs such structures are often seen as a problem, creating blind spots for a congregation—but not for a clown, for whom they present fantastic opportunities. It is so much more fun to peep round a pillar and gradually come out, and then disappear again.

This must have been one of the very first times that I told the Valentine story in a regular Sunday service. The church was full, and in addition to those who were sitting in the seats there could have been easily another hundred very small children clustered around the dais in the chancel. They were all eager to see "what was in the box." "The box" must have been the Mark One baby box—one of those cantilevered containers that unfolds as the lid is raised, and which had originally been used to carry around spare changes of clothing and other essential items when my own children were small. But now it had been covered in fluorescent pink plastic to turn it into a suitably garish container for my face paints and all Valentine's other bits and pieces. Someone told me later that as I opened the lid and peeped inside, it was as if a great wave of children all rose on tiptoe to see what would be revealed. It didn't take me long to realize that this was a great bonus. Small children sometimes appear frightened when suddenly confronted with a ready-made clown wearing funny clothes and makeup. It takes time to gain their confidence. It has been suggested that children already recognize the underlying connotations of a death mask in the white face, and this is what frightens them even though they would not be able to articulate it. Seeing the white makeup actually applied to Valentine's face, and then the colors and clothes being added, helps to demystify it all for them. I have also used this same technique on an individual basis to help children who have genuine fears of clowns, by visiting them in their homes and then giving them the chance to play with the makeup and other things before seeing me apply it to myself. This kind of play therapy seems to have been effective in helping them to overcome their fear.

But back to the service, which was an intergenerational event, something that in itself encouraged me enormously for all sorts of other reasons. The attention of the huge number of pre-school children was firmly held by the visual impact of what was going on, but the central message of Valentine drawing the crosses on her eyes and inviting the congregation to join her on the journey of faith gave the adults and older children more than enough to engage them.

Maintaining a wide appeal like this is crucial. All-age, or what are sometimes misleadingly called "family" services, have the potential for being really good experiences or absolutely dreadful occasions. In that respect, of course, they are just like any other kind of service. Probably the best services I have ever shared in have been all-age services, but equally some of the very worst services I have attended have also been all-age events. The problem usually arises when we assume that because we have all ages together we need to work with whatever we imagine to be the lowest common denominator—an approach that adults (and more especially teenagers) find to be embarrassing and unhelpful. I have never understood why we do this. When a baby arrives in a home, we gradually change things to include them and facilitate their development. We move precious ornaments out of harm's way into safe places, and tend to buy furnishings and clothes that can easily be washed. Going for the lowest common denominator of behavior might suggest that, since two-year-olds tip their breakfast cereal on their heads, everyone else should do the same. We can all see the absurdity of that in the home, but in the church we don't always apply the same logic. There is enormous value in the whole of God's people worshipping together. This is where our children will learn something about the experience of faith at work—not by sitting listening "how to," but by doing it with us as members of the community of faith.

Australia

It was as a result of sharing some of these thoughts as we walked through the Scottish countryside with Raymond Fung, Evangelism Secretary at the World Council of Churches, that John and I were first invited to go to Australia to take part in a three-week School of Evangelism in Adelaide for leaders from around the world, hosted by the WCC as part of the preparations for the 1991 Canberra Assembly.

This was a huge challenge for me. Up till now, a foray across "the border" was the extent of my world travel. But this was to be the start of what was to become the equivalent of the apostolic "Jerusalem . . . Samaria . . . and to the ends of the earth" (Acts 1:8), though I had no idea of that at the time. We packed to go with our two younger children, and as the plane touched down in Adelaide at six in the morning, the cold grey skies drenched with drizzle could easily have meant we had landed back in Scotland. A crumpled seven-year-old uncurled herself from having slept on top of me most of the way and announced in a pathetic voice, "I want to go home." Why did all our fellow travellers laugh? It didn't seem funny to me, though I knew how she felt. As we watched the eager expressions of those who were scanning the crowd for the familiar faces of well-loved relatives and friends, greeting them with warm embraces, and then leaving for their final destinations, it suddenly dawned on me that I was in a strange land and I didn't know a solitary soul.

At last, when virtually no one else was left, a young woman decided we must be the strangers she was looking for, introduced herself and drove us to our destination. What an odd place we were hosted in—a theological college with what felt like a three-mile hike to the nearest bathroom, up two flights of stairs and round lots of corners. Doing it with a seven-year-old in the middle of the night, and getting there in time, became quite an art form, I can tell you. I also soon learned that Australians don't believe in winter, and behave as if it's never cold in their climate. I just wish they had warned me in advance, because it was cold—and wet—even by Scottish standards. But we weren't the worst off by any means, for many of the others had travelled from much warmer places. Someone eventually went to the Salvation Army charity shop, who donated bundles of warm clothing to those who had journeyed from the non-Western world. Yet God moves in mysterious ways, and the austerity of the venue just encouraged the formation of even deeper friendships. I am still in touch with many of the people I met there.

Raymond Fung had put a lot of work into the organization, and his thinking translated what might have been a very average conference into something quite special. One of the most memorable aspects of the occasion was the many case studies and personal stories that were brought from around the world. One of the people I remember best was a young pastor from Malaysia, the Rev. An Men Tee—partly because he had such an impact on our son Mark, who was just twelve at the time. If I remember rightly, he had been a pastor for only a very few years in Malaysia, and had grown a church from nothing to several thousands. In a totally unselfconscious way, as though this happened everywhere, he described his experience of God at work in his community, and in particular spoke about many instances of healing. He probably imagined that this was nothing unusual either, but those of us from the West knew differently.

I think I know why Jesus took that child and set her in the midst (Mark 9:33-37), because when we came home and people asked the children how they had enjoyed their trip, Mark told everyone he met about this pastor in particular. More than that, he wanted to know why what An had described seemed not to be happening in Britain, and he kept asking different people with the tenacity (or stubbornness) of a twelve-year-old boy, because he didn't feel he was getting a satisfactory answer. He could probably have coped better with an honest "I don't know," but I was glad people asked him because even when I told them about the conference I didn't usually also ask the twelve-year-old's question. What was it that I commented on, several thousand words back, about Jesus having the capacity to affirm and then move on to challenge?

Barni had not been born at that stage, but I did share my story of Valentine in Adelaide. I also led some workshops in dance. Before I left Scotland, my friend Liz had been teaching me some movements to the song "I give you all the honor," the chorus of which includes the line "I give myself to you . . ." As she looked at my feeble attempt to stretch out my arms, elbows tucked into my waist, she said, "You can't give yourself to God like that: is that how you give a present, hanging on to it?" My body was obviously informing my words of the reality that I was, at that point, hanging on to much of myself and not offering it up to God. Every time I teach this song and dance, I share that experience, because it taught me so much about myself.

I certainly needed that counsel before I went to Adelaide and taught the delegates the dance in one of the workshops. The third verse in particular goes on to mention the way in which the gospel can release captives from whatever might hold them prisoner. As we sang the first line, we knelt in a circle with our hands above our heads as though in handcuffs, and as we moved on to celebrating the freedom offered by Christ, we dramatically broke the chains and swung our arms apart. At the opposite side of the circle to me was the Rev. Wesley Mabuza, a Methodist minister from South Africa. Remember, this was in 1990, when the apartheid system was still very much in place and the possibility of reform seemed a distant dream. He had been put in prison on numerous occasions simply because his skin was the wrong color and he was in the wrong place. His house had been raided by the police and his family threatened. Being a Christian minister had not protected him, but had actually led to even greater victimization than he might otherwise have encountered. Three times a year, every year for the preceding ten years, he had applied to get an exit visa to allow him to attend Christian conferences in other countries, and until now his applications had always been turned down. The evening before, we had all sat together and watched the film Cry Freedom, the story of Steve Biko's brutal treatment and death at the hands of the South African security forces. This film had been banned in South Africa, which meant that it was the first time Wesley had ever seen it, and many tears had flowed, from all of us. One of the most special moments of my entire life came as we sang, "You have broken chains that bound me": just watching Wesley's face conveyed far more to the rest of us than he could ever have described in any number of words. Words were painful, but the movement to the song created space for an extraordinary explosion of pent-up emotion from all the suffering that he and his people had borne, and sheer jubilation as he then sang, "You've set this captive free." Giving expression to all that emotion was healing for him, and inspirational and empowering for the rest of us. It would actually have been an injustice in itself not to have created the space that allowed him to express that response to God, and we would have been the poorer for not sharing his story in movement and feeling.

On that occasion, I went on to Melbourne and Perth, working either alone or alongside John with churches and other mission organizations involved especially with young people. Often we were invited to talk about the opportunities that had been created by the garden festival in Glasgow, and others were encouraged and inspired to look for new ways of doing things in their own context. It's important for us to share our stories with each other around the world, but it is just as important not to imagine that we can or should copy something just because it seems to be a good idea—or to imagine that a concept that worked in one place will automatically be appropriate somewhere else. Churches waste much energy in this way. It is, rather, important to identify where God is at work in our own communities and come alongside there, prayerfully and expectantly.

Although listening to someone else's story of faith might not provide a ready-made program for our own situation, this kind of sharing will nevertheless frequently act as a mirror or a prism that can shed light on different circumstances and help us find new directions for ourselves. I suppose this is what is called "lateral thinking." Women are regularly expected to do it all day long as they manage dozens of different demands on their lives at once. Children also intuitively do it all the time as they play. Men might have to work a bit harder at it, but they too have creative capacities reflecting the image of God, that can be nurtured and developed in relation to spirituality.

One of my most treasured memories of that first trip "down under" is a Sunday morning service at a church in Yokine, a suburb of Perth, Western Australia. It was an important day for the Girls' Brigade, and the area commissioner and various other important people and local celebrities were all there. I can't now remember what their official business was on that occasion, but I do still have a letter that came to me the next day after the service. It was from one of the church leaders, who told me that her teenage son, who was generally turned off by church and had not attended for some time, had come on that day, and as he listened to my story and engaged with the clown prayers and other things that happened, he had begun to see new possibilities for how Christian faith could engage with his life: "If only church was like this all the time." Sadly, I've lost count of the number of times I must have heard that comment, not just in Australia of course, for British churches are no different.

The World Comes to Scotland

Another WCC School of Evangelism took place about two years later. This time it was in Scotland, in the lovely setting of Stirling University on the Airthrey estate, once the home of the Haldane family who in their day did much to promote the gospel, not only in Scotland but in other parts of the world. It was therefore an appropriate location for a school of evangelism. I had suggested that June would be a good month, because the weather in Scotland is often at its best then. Well, it was: it poured with rain almost continuously for the entire two weeks. The first two days had been planned as a recreational opportunity for people to get to know one another, and this included sightseeing trips to the Scottish Highlands as well as sailing in a steamship on Loch Katrine in the Trossachs, which was so stormy that we mostly huddled together below decks to keep warm.

In retrospect, though, the weather was not the most significant thing. Again, the lessons we all learned were what made it special, particularly the stories that were shared across the cultural boundaries. Though I look back and laugh about it now, I recall one especially scary tale that came out as we were sitting having a drink in a local bar. The one thing that overseas visitors to Scotland can always be guaranteed to ask for is a visit to a pub to taste whisky. To accommodate a variety of different preferences, we went to a hotel where whisky was on sale, but those who did not want to drink alcohol were also in a pleasant atmosphere and could have soft drinks. I found myself sitting next to a church leader from Burma, who was on his third whisky when he turned to me and said: "I used to drink whisky a lot. Before I became a Christian, I was a head hunter and I always drank three whiskeys before I went out to kill." I'd never been so grateful for the grace of God either before or since!

But there was one moment during that conference which moved me even more profoundly than that. We spent quite a lot of time experiencing worship from many cultures, rather than just talking about this in sessions, and I had the task of preparing worship one evening. This also helped to fill in the wet evenings. I had decided to use a visual aid that I had found very moving on other occasions—a tree trunk placed in the middle of the floor with hammers and large nails around it. If you ever decide to do this for yourself, it is important to use a hefty branch and not a small log or twigs. We used the tree as a focus for prayer: people were invited to pray and, if they wished, to come and hammer in a nail as a symbol of the pain (or whatever) they wished to leave there. Since I had planned for this well in advance, I could hardly have anticipated that on the very day we used this form of prayer, the apartheid laws in South Africa would finally be repealed. One of the participants was Bishop Eric Pike, at that time Bishop of Grahamstown. This white South African bishop came into the midst of our circle and knelt by the tree for a long time. The place was silent except for some sobs, and then in due course three black Africans from different parts of the continent came and knelt with him and placed their arms around him. Believe me, the sobs were not restricted to those kneeling in the center. It was truly a place of repentance and new life, as Bishop Eric wept for the oppression of black South Africans by people who were not only the same color as himself but also claimed to be Christians, and equally the black sisters and brothers showed us the kind of grace and forgiveness that mirrored so perfectly the One we knew had been nailed to a tree in our place to deal with all injustices and bring peace to our troubled world.

Another participant at that conference was a worker among university students in Egypt. He found it hard going because he was not communicating in his first language. I engaged with him and shared meals on several occasions, although our conversation was sometimes a struggle. I was therefore very encouraged when I got a letter from him after he had returned home. "I write this letter from Alexandria," he said, "where last night I taught my church how to use the clown sketch I got from you. We enjoyed it during one of our worship times. Thank you, Olive—we learned a lot from you . . ." What he was referring to was the heart sketch again, described in appendix 2. One thing was certain: I could never have communicated the message in words, but mime had given us a common language. Not only that, but he had taken it back to his country, set it in an Egyptian context in a way that I would not have known how to do, and as a result the message of God's love had been shared in a place where I had not been. I find it very exciting to be in partnership with a God who works in this kind of cross-cultural way.

Chapter 6

Jamaica: Learning from the Poor

Most of what is worth knowing about the arts—and spirituality—
can be learned not by thinking but by doing things. As the theologians of liberation have taught us to recognize, praxis comes
before reflection. But sometimes the most significant learning
comes from unexpected quarters, which is why I am including
this chapter in the book. Though it does include some account of
my clown ministry, that is not the main focus here. It is a story
worth telling, not just because it is a good story, but more especially because the experiences I describe opened up for me what
was ultimately to become a more profound understanding of the
theology of clowning, if not of the entire basis of my Christian
spirituality.

In 1995, John and I were invited to go to Jamaica to lead a
conference on renewal of worship, organized by the United
Church of Jamaica and Cayman, but open to clergy of all
denominations. Historically, the Church of Scotland had close
links with Jamaica, sending many missionaries from Scotland in
the past. We will always be grateful that the church here made it
financially possible for us to go, because our own faith was challenged and, though they would not have thought it possible, we
must have learned at least as much from the Jamaican Christians
as we were able to share with them. In addition to speaking at
the conference, we spent some time in different parishes in

Jamaica, so that we could return with an informed view of what was going on there, which in turn might help the church back in Scotland to identify new ways of supporting and empowering their witness.

With all the plans drawn up, we almost never made it to Jamaica. Just 24 hours before we were due to go, our second son, Mark, fell ill and had to be hospitalized to have his appendix removed. Obviously, we had serious misgivings about going, and discussed whether only one of us should make the trip—though in reality neither of us alone could have carried through all the aspects of the program we had planned. The surgeon assured us that it would all be fine because Mark was young and would recover with no problems—but then, he was the doctor and not the parent.

The Jamaican Christians sent us a fax saying they were sorry to hear about our predicament, and assuring us that they had contacted all the churches throughout the island, who were now praying for Mark. Well, that boy felt like a million dollars—and not for the first time did he observe that "church" in the non-Western world seems to have a different way of expressing itself. This must surely have contributed to his speedy recovery, and certainly was a positive affirmation for a teenager growing in faith. In addition, the church leaders came up with a happy practical solution: the conference itself was not scheduled to start till a week later, and so we were able to switch things around, flying out in time for the conference and doing the parish visits afterwards. Some unexpected advantages emerged out of that rescheduling. Not only did our new flights cost less than the original ones, but our tickets were upgraded as well—every passenger's dream, and the only time it has ever happened to us. Having any extra baggage allowance is always valued when Barni and Valentine travel with us. One of these days I am going to face some extraordinary questioning if my luggage is examined. I can just hear it: "Is this really your makeup, ma'am? Do you normally wear a wig like this? These are your shoes?"

Ourselves the Way Others See Us

We touched down in Jamaica and stayed for our first night at a retreat house in Kingston belonging to the United Church. Another guest staying there was a tall blond Norwegian youth who seemed pleased to meet other Europeans, and chatted amiably with us. He had taken time out to travel and find the meaning of life, and had arrived in Jamaica in order to visit the home of the singer Bob Marley, which was just nearby. He was curious to know what we were doing. I can't remember exactly how we described ourselves, but when the term "New Age" cropped up in our conversation, his eyes lit up. Like many in the West, he was obviously a spiritual searcher—and no doubt if we had said we were there on a fact-finding mission for the Church of Scotland, he would have had little or no further interest. In sharing faith effectively with such people, we need to be able to pick up on their starting-points, and that usually means listening first.

We talked with him on several occasions, but were unable to journey with him for long. We have to trust that we were just a link in the chain of faith that was being made for him and that others on the journey will have helped him to incorporate other links.

A young woman called Jet den Hollander had collected us from the airport, and she was our minder throughout our stay in Kingston. Originally from the Netherlands, she had obviously adapted enthusiastically to Jamaican life, driving us with ease through the crowded streets, which often had undefined edges to the roads, not to mention potholes and huge amounts of traffic, people and animals all jumbled together. Our first visit to the denominational headquarters to meet those who had invited us was filled with anticipation and excitement—on both sides. Don't imagine the kind of place where denominational bureaucrats in Britain might be based. This was a smallish building, with offices on the ground floor and a recording studio upstairs, all in a yard at the back of one of the downtown churches. In Western terms, this would class as a basic facility, certainly cramped in relation to the number of people who worked there and the amount of work they did. But they knew how to make a little go a very long way.

Like most churches in Jamaica, this one also had a school alongside it, and as we looked around the premises hundreds of primary school children squealed with excitement at seeing us. They didn't often see a white person and I think we looked very white indeed, arriving from Scotland in February. I remember thinking how incredibly handsome and happy these Jamaican children looked, their faces all shining eagerly to see us. I joined them in one of the classrooms—a place with none of the equipment you would expect to find in a school in Britain, and where the main educational resource was obviously the teacher and the kids themselves. They all worked at long, low tables, and as I sat down for a moment my medium-sized frame dwarfed the chair I was on. They crushed around me, eager to show off their neat writing, and delighted by the praise I gave them. For me, it was definitely love at first sight. I have never forgotten my meeting not only with these children, but with many others throughout the island. In fact, a line drawing of a child by the famous Jamaican artist J. Macdonald Henry hangs on the stairway of my house, so I pass it many times a day, and as I do so I regularly pray for those children and that impoverished country.

A smart five-year-old, immaculately dressed in his cotton school uniform, pushed himself on to my knee, took hold of my cheeks firmly, one in each hand, and said, "You have a face just like a monkey." I knew at the time that there was absolutely no intended insult in this statement. He was just comparing me to what he knew, and that was the nearest thing he could think of. I remembered my Scottish roots, and the famous lines from Robert Burns's poem, "To a Louse":

O wad some Pow'r the giftie gie us
To see oursels as others see us!
It wad frae mony a blunder free us,
And foolish notion.

Everywhere we went in Jamaica, no matter what time of day it was, we seemed to see children in eye-catching, colorful school uniforms, girls with skirts and blouses and boys in short trousers and short-sleeved shirts. Different schools had different colors: blue and white, pink, green and yellow. We subsequently discovered that the reason they could be seen walking to and from school at all hours throughout the day was because resources are so limited that most children cannot be in class for a whole day, and so one group of children will go in the morning and another group in the afternoon. Education is highly prized and has to be paid for by everyone, with even the poorest families doing everything in their power to make sure their children get some schooling. The vast majority of schools seemed to have some church connection, and we felt that this was one of the most significant contributions being made to the life of their people by the Jamaican Christian community.

The day after our arrival, we left Kingston to go to the Madge Saunders Conference Center at Ocho Rios, in the north-eastern corner of the island. The journey itself was interesting, not only because it gave us the chance to see at first hand the beautiful scenery in the heart of this lush green island, but also and more especially because it gave us an insight into the lifestyle of many Jamaican people. The bus itself was quite an experience, with no air-conditioning and a very strong smell of diesel fumes. At times it felt as if it had no springs either, and the road hardly helped, with an abundance of hairpin bends—all of which the driver negotiated at the same speed as he had driven along the straight bits of road. At many places there were simple wood and grass shelters where people had set up stalls to sell local fruit and drinks.

A Different Level of Commitment

The conference center itself was an impressive complex, situated alongside a school which was also operated by the local church. Madge Saunders, after whom it was named, was a former

Moderator of the General Assembly of the United Church. She had a particular vision to reach out to the children and young people of Jamaica, and saw that a key way of doing this would be through the establishment of a residential center where camps and retreats could be held. As often happens when councils and committees of churches are invited to support work among young people, she came up against a degree of lethargy and lack of interest in her project. Frustrated by red tape and bureaucracy, she determined to do something about it, and so she sold one of her own most valuable possessions, took the proceeds with her to a committee meeting, and tipped them out of her bag on to the table with the words, "This is my contribution to help finance this center: what are you going to do about it?" Her bold action unblocked the system, the center was procured, and the other church leaders got the message about risk-taking and steps of faith—and named the center after her!

For us, the mere fact that we had been asked at all to lead this conference was one of the most challenging and empowering aspects of the experience. We were more conscious here than we have been in any other non-Western country that it was our forebears who in so many ways had been the oppressors of the Jamaican people. Though it was not our fault, and we were well removed in time from the worst excesses of colonialism, we certainly felt a sense of corporate responsibility and guilt that is hard to explain. But we also found ourselves overwhelmed by what we understood as grace and forgiveness on the part of these wonderful people who were so open to what we had to share with them in their conference.

Valentine and Barni had both travelled packed in my suitcase. During the conference, Barni shared communion with these beautiful warmhearted people, for whom the sight of a hobo in the street was an everyday thing—indeed, it was common to see people not only begging on the streets, but actually living on a patch of pavement they had claimed as "home," cooking on a tiny stove if they were fortunate enough to have one. So the figure of Barni unpacking the apparent pickings from the rubbish, and from the dross and dirt sharing a crust of bread and someone's discarded wine, was almost physically overpowering even though no words were spoken. As the conference participants shared the bread and wine together, I needed to move out of the way and give them space to be with God. Leaving the room, where people were praying and ministering to one another, Barni almost bumped into Maitland Evans, the conference organizer and general secretary of the United Church, who was himself in deep reflection behind a pillar in the passageway that led to the grounds outside. As we met, he said nothing, but reverently placed his hands together in a position of prayer and bowed. It was another sign of thanks, of affirmation, of forgiveness, of blessing, of ordination and more, and Barni returned the bow in silence—while God continued to speak to both of us.

One of the things that the Jamaican Christians needed us to do perhaps more than anything else was to give them permission to do new things in worship. In some ways, they had allowed themselves to become locked in a timewarp, preserving the styles of worship and witness given to them by our forebears when they first went there. A group from Guyana were insistent that the only hymn book worth using was one compiled in Scotland in the 1920s, which the missionaries of a previous generation had shared with them. They were puzzled to hear that the church in Scotland had abandoned that one long ago, and couldn't understand how that had been possible without also losing some essential components of the faith. It wasn't particularly easy for us to deal with this. On the one hand, we could see that we carried considerable authority because we too had come from Scotland, and yet we could see how the easy adoption of practices from our culture had in the past had the effect of inhibiting the natural cultural response of these people to the gospel. We were reluctant to make the same mistake again, and resisted it at first. As we talked with them, though, it became obvious that, for some Christians, it was actually important to be given permission to change by people of the same ethnic origin as those who had originally established their churches. So we found ourselves regretting the way these wonderfully creative people had been disempowered, while realizing that it was now up to us to do what we could to help them move forward, at the same time making sure that we would not impose our own values and opinions on them in ways that could just lock them into our own timewarp.

The original inhabitants of Jamaica were entirely wiped out by European colonists, and the present population is all of African descent, taken there in the first place to work as slaves on the many plantations. Like all Africans, they loved dancing: it was a natural part of their inherited culture, and exploring it in a context of worship was something they found both novel and worthwhile. Unlike Western people, they had few inbuilt inhibitions about moving around, either in church or elsewhere, and once they realized that this could be a way to redeem part of the culture, they entered into it with great enthusiasm. Another thing they loved doing was Bible study using a technique I have come to describe as "Bible Stills," and which is described in detail in appendix 1 at the end of this book. Since we were also thinking about mission, one evening we had some visitors who were not part of any church come to dialogue with us. One of them was a Rastafarian, whom I found especially intriguing because he delivered his entire address using drums, and singing what he had to say. That seemed to sum up for me the kind of problem most of our churches now face. In a culture where the preferred methods of communication include so many different media, we still seem happiest to stick with words. And of course, that is the culture in Britain, every bit as much as in a place like Jamaica.

On the Sundays of our visit, John and I each visited different churches. I went to a small church in a village where the streets were dust tracks and the church was about the most substantial building around. Not that it was at all grand, for it consisted of a wooden shack with no glass for windows, and I don't remember seeing any doors on the entrance either. In some ways it reminded me of the Glasgow mission my father had worked in when I was a really small child. The benches were certainly the same pattern, and the congregation all gathered in their best clothes. I really enjoyed their love of color and spectacle. Despite their obvious poverty, many of the women and girls were wearing clothes of the kind that we in Britain would wear to a special occasion like a wedding. So I did not feel at all out of place in my bright pink clown costume, sequined tailcoat, over-sized clown shoes, multi-colored wig and white gloves. Had I gone in my regular Sunday clothes, I might have felt a bit underdressed for the occasion! But my hosts were delighted to see me and took me off down the village street to greet other people in their homes who had not come to church. Some of the congregation stood in the middle of the village and sang and invited those looking on with interest to come and join them in the church for worship. A significant number emerged to see what was going on, and of course sent their children out when they saw the clown. Valentine gave them each a balloon printed with a heart and the slogan "God loves you," and some of them came back with us to the church.

As the service got under way, I was surprised to realize that the entire event was being led by the children, the vast majority of whom would have been primary school age. They did absolutely everything, and did it all with great confidence and expertise. The children had created their own rap version of a Bible passage, and then two girls who must have been about eleven years old had worked out some movement to a song, while the announcements were delivered by a boy of about ten— and all with great care and attention to detail. Much to their delight, Valentine clowned and gave away more balloons, while some who had been at the conference presented one of their Bible Stills, based on the story of the Good Samaritan. Valentine also did the heart mime mentioned in Chapter 4, and here again the ability for mime to reach across cultures and ages was evident. The children and the adults picked up my "heart" and threw it back—this was an occasion on which I had to work solo—but they understood what was going on very quickly. Their response told me that.

On our way back to the conference center, one of the ministers told me about the "anansi," a traditional mischief-maker in

Jamaican culture, and wondered if there would be some connection between this character and the clown image that could be exploited in order to contextualize the gospel more effectively. It was seeing Valentine operating in the street, in a mission context, that had highlighted the possibility of perhaps creating a culturally relevant character that could feature in her outreach work.

On the final evening of the conference, people from different Caribbean islands shared something of their culture, to everyone's delight and sometimes amusement. I learned some of their beautiful dance movements and we had great fun trying to teach them a traditional Scottish dance, The Dashing White Sergeant. We ate a meal together that was very reminiscent of the Last Supper, as friends old and new shared many thoughts of our days together, made speeches and told stories as we reflected on what the coming of God's kingdom might mean for us—then Jet stood up and suggested we make a toast to God. It was something that Barni and Valentine could both have approved of, and was an appropriate way to express the unanimous thanks of all the participants for a great week of learning and sharing together. The most important guest at that table really was divine, after all.

Some of God's Very Special People

After the conference ended, we spent a second week in and around Montego Bay, one of the main tourist centers of Jamaica. Our guide this time was Margaret Fowler, a Scot who had originally gone there as a social worker, but who by this time was a United Church minister. The purpose of our visit was to see firsthand the life of a typical parish, and so we spent most of the time sharing in the everyday business of the church. Some things are the same the world over, and like many parishes in Britain this was a rural situation with a fairly scattered population and two church buildings where services were held regularly. Most visits had to be undertaken in a four-wheel-drive vehicle, as the terrain was rough and steep as well as being very extensive. Margaret had an interesting pastoral style, and whenever she spotted anyone she knew (or even, on occasion, people she didn't know), she just stopped and spoke with them. Around one corner we encountered a couple of teenage youths kicking a football. As we stopped the car, they came over to speak with us, and Margaret immediately asked them about their faith—and why they had not turned up at church to play their musical instruments for her, when they had promised to do so. They obviously held her in great respect, as they explained that they had gone off to play football instead, and apologized for that while promising that it would not happen again. We reflected on how teenagers in Britain might have responded to the same questions from a minister.

This parish also had a school attached to the church. While Margaret attended to some business with the head teacher, I sat outside. A little girl of about six, wearing a brightly patterned blue dress, eyed me up and down, and when I smiled she ran over and sat down alongside me before asking, "Would you like to see my school book? This is what I've done today." She was so proud of it, and as I chatted with her she told me all the little details of the day that are important to a girl of her age. It was such a happy encounter, and I found myself reflecting that in Britain and most other Western countries this kind of casual conversation simply wouldn't happen. We are constantly having to warn our children not to talk to strangers at all—and, if the boy in Kingston who thought I looked like a monkey was to be believed, then I must have seemed very strange indeed to her. The abuse of children in our own culture has deprived us of those special relationships that can be so uplifting to children and adults alike. Of course, I know that such things do go on in other cultures, and Jamaica will probably be no exception to that.

Another visit that sticks in my mind was to an old man living alone in a house on a hillside. Though small and cramped, his living-room was crammed with furniture, much of which reminded me of my own childhood—especially a display cabinet in the corner, of a design that could be found in every tenement in Glasgow when I was a child and in which fancy ornaments and other special things would be on display. In fact, it looked absolutely identical to the one my parents had and, given the colonial history of the place, it could quite possibly have originated in the very same Scottish factory. I wondered how it had come to be in this hillside dwelling on the other side of the world. As I sat next to him on a wooden seat a little higher than his sofa, I could see that the old man was very ill. The smell in his house was dreadful, as if the odor of death was already upon him even though he was still living. As we shared communion and prayed with him, we all recognized that we might be some of the last people to see him before he entered into God's greater presence.

We also visited a tin shack made of corrugated iron, which was home to a very poor couple with several children. They had become foster-parents to a boy of about seven, whose father lived in a nearby town and who had three other children whom he was struggling to look after following the death of their mother. He simply couldn't afford this small boy, whose name I can easily remember—Kirk. Though he seemed to have nothing, he took me on a tour of the patch of land outside the hut, proud to show me small clumps of vegetables he had planted here and there, which would make a valuable contribution to the family's economy. As we walked further afield among the trees and bushes, I realized that he had a considerable knowledge of many things, as he was able to identify a huge number of plants and tell me how they could be used for food or medicine. Like many bright children in such places all over the world, his opportunities for further education would be strictly limited. Taking kids like this out of their setting and educating them in other places wouldn't solve anything, but I was reminded how, in our interconnected world, the way we live in the West determines the quality of life such a child might enjoy.

Nightmares of the Colonial Legacy

Two other stories from this particular parish are worth including here. One place we visited was Rose Hall Plantation. Originally built in 1780, Rose Hall Great House is today one of the most prestigious tourist attractions in Jamaica, but its claim to fame—or notoriety—is connected to Annie Mae Patterson Palmer, wife of the last owner of the plantation, John Palmer. Annie had an unenviable reputation for witchcraft and brutality, and was said to be the daughter of an Irish missionary and a voodoo priestess, brought up in Haiti. The fact that her three husbands all died in mysterious circumstances only served to enhance her reputation as a person of magical powers, not to mention great cruelty. Standing that day in the grand rooms of this wonderful residence, I found it hard to believe the stories I was hearing—of how Annie Palmer would send for slaves to amuse her before dinner, regularly insisting they fought to the death for her pleasure; of how after dinner she would often send for a slave to have sex with her, and would then murder him. After instructing others to carry out the body for burial, she would push them too into the open grave and bury them alive, to conceal the evidence of her lifestyle. Eventually, when Annie and a slave girl both fell in love with the plantation supervisor, they invoked voodoo spells against one another in a battle that ended with a general slave uprising in 1831, in which Annie Palmer was killed and the sugar fields destroyed.

As I wandered round the magnificent grounds, with their metal traps to catch runaway slaves, and stood on the balcony from which Annie Palmer watched slaves mutilate one another for her amusement, which in turn was only a few steps away from the bedroom where she murdered so many, I could hardly help but be moved by the unimaginable cruelty of life in that place during the 1820s, when it was home to more than two thousand slaves, every one of whom must have been in fear for their life.

On another afternoon, we went to take a look at Mount Zion Church—just a bit further up the hillside overlooking Rose Hall. Like the plantation, Mount Zion was also a little bit of colonial history. What's more, it was Scottish colonial history, for it began life in Glasgow and the whole of its fabric and furniture was physically transported to Jamaica in the 1820s as ship's ballast. Slaves then spent several years of their spare time carrying the materials to the top of the hill, and reconstructing the church there. It must have been hard labor, for it took us forty minutes in a four-wheel-drive vehicle to get from sea level up to where the church now stands. Eventually, the work was completed: a little bit of Scotland in Jamaica, complete with pews, fancy lights—even slates on the roof. To celebrate its completion, and to acknowledge the hard work that had gone into it all, the minister responsible for getting it there gave the workers a reward. It was a bell that would call the people to worship, and inscribed on it was a verse of scripture: "Where the spirit of the Lord is, there is liberty" (2 Corinthians 3:17).

As I stood there, I recalled all the Marxist critiques of the missionary movement that I had come across, and had generally concluded were either untrue or at least certainly exaggerated. But now the evidence was undeniable, for it was there before my very eyes. No wonder I learned a lot on that trip—not only about how clown ministry could transcend cultural and ethnic boundaries, but also about how easy it is for us to take the gospel and turn it into an instrument of oppression. Right from the start, I had known that my ministry was about vulnerability, for it had grown out of my own weakness. I now started to reflect more precisely on the theological consequences of losing that focus, for it was my forebears who exported that church from Glasgow, obviously under the impression that they somehow owned God—that God would not be in Jamaica until the church had arrived. The meaning of "heresy" began to take on new dimensions for me.

Finally, back in Kingston we went on a quick trip to some of the more dangerous areas—places that Western tourists usually do their best to avoid, but with Maitland Evans as our guide we felt pretty safe. It gave us an interesting insight not only into Jamaican street culture, but more especially into the way that it was possible for Christians to minister effectively in that context, for Maitland was obviously well respected by even the toughest characters on the streets, who recognized his commitment to them and their environment. We also had one last purchase to make, not in a tourist shop but in a street market in the evening. Our son Mark had started buying distinctive hats from different countries when he was in Australia and obtained an akubra (a classic bush hat made from rabbit's fur). He had sent us off to Jamaica to find a Rastafarian hat to add to his collection. It wasn't hard to find one, though bartering for it took a bit longer.

The next day we would be flying home, and as we lay down to sleep (back in the church retreat center), we thought we had seen it all. The noise of city nightlife in Kingston never really eases off, but when a dog started to bark in a particularly agitated way in the house next door, I sensed something odd was happening. Sure enough, the next thing I heard was the sound of fighting and guns going off. It sounded as though the perpetrators were just on the other side of our bedroom wall (which was made of wood, albeit totally enclosed in a cage to keep robbers out). When I heard them whispering just outside the window, trying to decide what they might do next, I sat bolt upright in bed, shook John, and urged him in the quietest possible voice to "do something." This request was not well received, though I found it impossible to take his advice and lie down and go to sleep. My vivid imagination was overtaken with visions of never living to see Scotland or my children again, and when in due course I crept across the bedroom floor to the bathroom (which had only a wooden shutter, and no window) I was even more alarmed to hear that the intruders had moved round to there. It all seemed dangerously near me, though for Jamaicans it is part of everyday life—and death.

Still, when dawn came it was as if nothing had happened. John had slept, I didn't. We both had breakfast and bid our hosts farewell. We had been there just over two weeks, but I felt that I had had a lifetime's education in the process. My understanding of mission had been shifted to a new perspective, and I think that in some subtle way, not only Olive had changed as a result, but also Valentine and Barni had matured in the process.

Chapter 7

More Teaching and Learning

California—Here I Come!

A few years before the visit to Jamaica, we had started what was to become a regular pattern of our family lifestyle, as we visited California each summer for Christian ministry and to facilitate John's research into new spiritual movements. I first visited the west coast of America as a student in Berkeley, and I realized from the start that California is truly a melting pot of the world's cultures. When John and I became involved with Fuller Seminary in Pasadena, one of its attractions was the broad spectrum of students that it draws in, not only from the USA but from all around the world. The fact that its students study in different disciplines (the Fuller School of Psychology is one of the largest in California) is an additional benefit, and though we were based in the School of Theology the first course we taught there was deliberately interdisciplinary, which ensured that we met people with many different interests and concerns.

The course itself—called "Spirituality and Creativity for Worship and Evangelism"—emerged out of our experience of ministry and mission, and naturally included space for Valentine and Barni to play a significant role. Although John and I had both been to the US before, we felt that in stepping into this new space it was important for us to include in our teaching things that had been tried and tested on the ground. Even so, teaching a course on these subjects can never be restricted merely to head knowledge. We wanted to enable our students to explore risky space in a safe way, and discover what vulnerability might mean for them—all of it motivated by our own discovery that this is a fundamental part of personal preparation for ministry. Of course, what is true for students needs to be true for tutors as well. I think that being Valentine enables me to be true to that model of incarnation more fully.

Since 1992 we have taught this course several times as a summer intensive (forty hours over two weeks). This makes it more accessible to a greater number of students, and it's not uncommon for individuals to enroll because they think it looks like a soft option, only to discover in the process that God challenges their presuppositions. I remember being quite worried on my second visit to Pasadena when I met Brenda, a student from the previous year, who told me that she and her husband had decided to have a family after she took the class! At first, I was a bit alarmed and wondered what I might possibly have said to bring forth such a response—until she explained that I had commented in a throwaway remark that I had probably learned more from my own children than from anybody else, and she realized she might be missing out on something. She was right, of course, and I still believe that the spiritual journey with my children has nurtured me in very profound ways.

Students can—and do—attend seminary to learn how to run the church and keep the existing systems operational, but when your professor turns into a tramp clown halfway through a class, unpacks a bag of rubbish to reveal the bread and wine of communion, and then invites you to take part, you get a different message. I don't use this as an invitation for every seminary student to take up clowning, but it does challenge people to be serious about ministry and to realize that the heart of the matter is about entering into real-life situations. Practical theology is not about standing on the sidelines pontificating and splitting hairs about doctrine or exegesis.

One of the things I like most about American students is their honesty in expressing their opinions, because that also means that they are not daunted by being directly challenged to move forward in their own thinking. I remember using a liturgy that addressed the abuse of women by men. All the men in the class sat in a circle facing outward to a circle of women who surrounded them and faced inward. One young woman appreciated the physical layout, but disliked the words of the litany, which she felt seemed to implicate her as a victim, when she actually felt she had power over her life. I was able to say (truthfully), "Well, I didn't write this: it reflects the valid experience of abused women back in Scotland, who compiled this themselves. So we have to acknowledge its authenticity, and value it as coming from their life story." But I also felt free to say to her, "Why don't you go and write me one that will be true to life as you understand it?" Instead of feeling browbeaten, as many British people might have done, she went off and did exactly that—and presented me with a litany that I have used myself with other women in different situations.

Fun in God's House

Although this course was to be taught in partnership with John, we agreed from the outset that I would be the course designer. In working through this challenge, I wanted a course that was to be taught as a summer intensive to be different from the kind of thing theological students regularly encounter. For one thing, the longer time available each day provided opportunities for creative course design, as it seemed obvious to us that no one could be expected either to speak or to listen for four hours. In addition, many students were giving up their holiday time to attend, and it was appropriate that it should be fun as well as educational. As we later discovered, it turned out to be fun precisely because it was educational, while the pattern of four-hour sessions has revolutionized other teaching we have done both individually and together in different contexts.[4]

With ten days to play with, and the challenge of engaging creative Californians, who just love to experiment with new things, I decided to design this course on spirituality and creativity around the notion of God's house, and we would visit a different room each day. I had made this decision long before we discovered how serendipitous it was for Fuller Seminary, one of whose illustrious former professors, Robert Boyd Munger, had written a spiritual classic titled *My Heart—Christ's Home* (based on a sermon he preached in Berkeley as long ago as 1947).[5]

At the first class, we meet one another in the lobby, where we dump our baggage and compare notes about what we have each brought with us. It is always enlightening and challenging to realize how much baggage Christians bring with them, not only cultural but more especially religious and spiritual—and how much of a relief it can be to unpack it. Another day, we move into the living room, which is a place to share our stories. This is one of the key ways in which Christians can share their faith with postmodern people, but it is also a valuable tool in understanding ourselves. As we recall our own stories and tell them to others, we can perceive with new understanding what is going on in our lives—especially when others then tell them back to us. One of the particular things we like to do is to write stories for one another in this course and translate them into fairy stories where three hurdles have to be introduced and overcome before the written story is given back to the original teller.

In another room, we work on a collage, but not just any collage: this is a very personal thing. I usually invite people to make it in the shape of themselves—man or woman—not just bits of paper stuck randomly on a piece of card, and to include in it cuttings, clippings, stuff torn from papers, magazines and so on that represent different areas of their lives. Some have a natural aptitude for this sort of thing, while others find they have to work really hard at it. It's good for people training for ministry to be put into situations where they don't naturally excel: it enables them to understand just how useless people can feel in church if their own skills don't correspond to what the church thinks is valuable (which all too often is restricted to things that ministers and musicians might do).

Understood in that way, even apparently insignificant things like making a collage can lead to very important learning experiences. I shall never forget the first time I introduced this into a class at Fuller Seminary, not least because one student excelled, and produced a work of art of such superb quality that it has stuck with me ever since. He was absolutely in his element, and set about it like a workaholic. In fact, the class did this exercise one Friday morning, and at the end of the allotted time he said he would have to take his project home to continue working on it. When he returned the following Monday, his collage was about two feet square with the most intricate details defined within the shape of a man. Over the next few days, he continued to work on it, and eventually told me he had spent 48 hours in total. "This has just been a wonderful experience," he commented. "It has enabled me to express myself and resolve many areas of my thinking." Three or four years later, we caught up with him again. By then he had graduated and moved to another state but happened to be passing through California while I was there. "Do you remember my collage?" he asked—as if I could ever forget. "I have it laminated and it is in pride of place in my home." He went on to tell me that he was involved in a ministry with college students and was using this same technique as a tool to enable others to articulate their own spiritual search. That was exceptional. When other theological students make collages, the experience is not so profound—but they regularly see themselves in a new light when they take their work home. Their kids also relate to them differently when their parent's work is on the fridge door alongside their own.

On two days of this particular course we celebrated communion, once in the kitchen and then again in the dining room. There's always more than one way to do things—in fact, doing familiar things in unfamiliar ways regularly brings new insights. One of my favorite days is the last one—not just because I'm probably planning to go off for a well-earned break, but because we end with food, celebrating the time we have spent together and the journey that has taken place in our lives. With each one equipped with a slice of matzo (unleavened bread), we go and search out every other person in the class, break and share a piece with them and tell them how their life in the class has impinged on us. Then we share wine and encourage each other to know God's wholeness in our lives. This is a way of affirming one another—which is worth doing anyway—but it also serves to remind us how Jesus related to people, always lifting them up and valuing them before anything else. Too many people experience church as the opposite of this, and find themselves put down by those who—of course—tell them it is "in love." We do not model Jesus's example of community this way. In fact that kind of negative behavior can often discourage those who are seriously searching for spiritual meaning (see John 13:34-35).

Inevitably, God's house has a bathroom, and we visit there too. All children love to play with water, including theology students—and finding the child within ourselves is one of the most urgent tasks for those who would be effective in Christian mission in the 21st century. The opportunity for cleansing is offered through water in all the Christian traditions, though often this is restricted to baptism. Jesus never baptized anyone, but he certainly used water. For example, he washed his disciples' feet (John 13:1-11), which points to the potential of having water readily available when we meet for worship, so that people can either wash their own hands or indeed offer to wash someone else's feet or hands, or make the sign of the cross on one another—or whatever their imagination might inspire them to do. Washing one another, in whatever way it is done, requires a reciprocal giving and taking from both parties. Ministers in particular are often very happy to give, but can find it much harder to receive.

Fresh Angles on Church

Although my regular visits to southern California have been at the invitation of Fuller Seminary, I have visited and taken part in many different churches there too. I remember going to a student apartment at the invitation of one of my Fuller students. He had been so moved in class by Barni's Feast that he wanted his church to share the experience. Their regular time for church was a mid-week evening. By British standards it was an informal group: some were students, others were friends who lived in the neighborhood, while others came in small groups from the places where they worked, either full-time or part-time. There must have been about thirty people crowded into a couple of rooms—all of them young people, in their twenties and thirties—and music was provided by a CD player and accompanied by the burning of a joss stick for incense. It was a memorable occasion, not just because of the surroundings, nor because Barni was there, but especially because one of the group was moving away to go to a new job. This person had been struggling to survive, and when the group first met him he was a dropout with few prospects. But through their friendship he had found new faith and fresh support, and now for the first time in his life it seemed as if things were going right for him. There were many tears as they said their farewells and produced a big party cake for him, which meant that we ate something sacramental twice that night—the cake and the bread of Barni's mime.

At the opposite end of the spectrum—socially, ecclesiastically, and in every other way you care to imagine—was a movie director who invited me to go to his church in Hollywood. This was an Episcopal church, led by a Hispanic priest who I think was much more conservative than he wanted to admit and was slightly worried about me at first, and what I might do with his service. In the event, though, we hit it off really well in personal terms. Valentine was deemed to have made a worthwhile contribution to the Sunday morning Eucharist, and I was invited to return any time I am in Hollywood.

On one trip back from New Zealand, I was invited to take the services in Hawaii, at University Avenue Baptist Church in Honolulu. It is the only church where I have preached in my bare feet and felt that this was the right way to be. We were welcomed with wonderfully fragrant garlands of ginger flowers, and one of the things I enjoyed most about that congregation was the very wide cross-section of the population who felt welcomed there. Ordinary people from the community sat alongside students, a judge and the head of a school—and it was impossible for me to tell one from the other until they introduced themselves. We also had lunch under the trees after the service. It was the fifth anniversary of the founding of a Vietnamese church who shared their building. Many of the older people still had very little English, so there was a service for them in their own language. Since I never was much good at languages at school, being a clown is wonderful because I get to gesticulate and use my hands and mime, and I'm never stuck for words—so I had a ball with the Vietnamese kids.

On the BBC

You might think that, having been to all these places, there would be little else to report from the 1990s. But of course to the British establishment you've never been anywhere until you've been on the BBC. When I was invited to do three programs for them, I expected it to be an interesting challenge, and so it was. Once I got to know him, the producer was a great help to me, though our first meeting reminded me of just how incredibly stiff the British can be. He arranged to visit me at my home, and shortly after the time he was expected he called to say that he would be late as he was at a police station, having had a "slight accident" with his car. Since I'd never met him before, I had no way of knowing if he looked pale when he arrived, but he was certainly brisk and businesslike and launched straight into his agenda.

Only gradually did I begin to realize that his briefcase was full of water, and it slowly dawned on me that his shoes were caked in mud, but it was not until he stood up to leave, and saw the puddle beneath him, that he admitted his trousers were soaking—and the full story emerged. His "slight accident" had happened when the steering on the car he had rented locked solid, which caused him to career right across the road, through a fence and into a ditch that was full of water and had obviously flooded the car. But being quintessentially of the "stiff upper lip" disposition, he had rented a second car and stoically proceeded to our meeting almost as if nothing had happened.

So I knew from the beginning that this would be a different sort of experience, with interesting people to work with. Writing the programs became a real challenge for me. As you will know by now, having read this far, I am not short of words, but in clowning I am so accustomed to having to think on my feet in churches and on the streets that keeping to a script can be a particular problem. The camera crew who worked with me were among the most patient guys I've come across. They needed to be, for when the appointed time to do the recordings arrived, it turned out that the whole of Britain was in deep mourning for Diana, Princess of Wales, whose sudden death had shaken the entire nation not long before.

With more of an eye for spectacle than sensitivity, the program makers thought it would be a great idea for me to clown in the square of a major English city, surrounded by the many tributes to Princess Diana which were everywhere. I had enough clowning experience to understand how and when you can approach people, and I kept telling them it wouldn't work because people were in mourning. But they were the BBC, and infinitely wiser than a clown. We did go into the city center, I engaged with some children and their parents, laughed with those who were laughing, and waved from a distance to people drinking coffee on the sidewalk. But it was all quite low key—not a disaster, just understated. I was not at all surprised—it was an excellent example of the clown needing to be vulnerable, and only stepping into someone's psychological space at their invitation. Holman Hunt displays this concept in another art form in his famous painting of Christ knocking at the heart's door, whose only handle is on the inside. Jesus never forced his way into anyone's life, and the Christian clown must always follow his example.

There were other memorable moments as well. The director found the underlying message of Valentine quite hard to handle, and felt that the simple invitation to come and see the world the way God sees it was not quite powerful enough. Obviously exasperated by me, she eventually exploded with, "Can't you beef up the cross a bit?" There are times in life when words simply aren't enough, and this was one such occasion. Mime skills were especially useful, and my response was to make my eyebrows disappear into my hairline—while mentally recalling another episode when Jesus found it inappropriate to give a verbal response to his questioner (see John 8:1-11).

In spite of all that, the two programs showing Valentine were certainly worth making, though a third program that would have featured Barni had to be dropped because of the way the TV schedules were disrupted by coverage of events surrounding Princess Diana's death. Paradoxically, though, it was Barni who underwent the most development as a result of all this, and the character took a great leap forward because of the program the BBC never made. Up until this point Barni had never spoken, but had always been a silent mime. In order to make a television program, I had to find out from within what sort of things Barni would say, and how all the things symbolized by a tramp clown might be articulated. As a result of that, I was able to develop Barni's character so that she can talk to absolutely anyone. There is no need for others to ask questions or answer back, though if they do that's not a problem. But Barni just speaks, commenting on what is going on, reflecting on the meaning of things, producing throwaway remarks that are often more profound than I realize at the time.

PART 2

The Meaning
of It All

Chapter 8

Spiritual Reflections

In this chapter and the next one, I want to revisit some of the episodes that I have already described, by way of further reflection on the meaning of it all. Here I will share some comments on what I call the "spiritual" dimensions of clowning, by which I mean those things that have moved me in such a way as to enable me to become a different—hopefully better—person. Then in the next chapter I will move on to some more specifically theological reflections—recognizing that theology should always inspire personal transformation, while our personal spirituality should both inform and shine through our theological expressions. This is the "praxis-reflection-renewed praxis" model of doing theology that has been inspiring the world church for almost half a century now, and which more recently has turned the world of so-called "practical theology" upside down. Now that you have been introduced to my multi-faceted spiritual journey into the world of Christian clown ministry, your own reflections on what you have read thus far will equip you better to engage with this process than if I had introduced it in an earlier chapter.

"I am having a clown workshop weekend sometime soon: I think you should come." I suppose that invitation, given to me by Philip Noble at the end of an afternoon's fun during the mission already mentioned in chapter 1, was the gateway to my first real encounter with clown ministry. Though I have never asked him, I have often wondered why Philip invited me. His own clowning grew from his love of stories and string art, skills nurtured in his early years of ministry as a priest in Papua New Guinea.[6] In the light of his own sense of professionalism, maybe I seemed so hopeless that he felt I needed some essential training, and fast—though in reality, as Philip mentored me over the following years, I came to realize that his comment had clearly arisen out of his sense of spiritual discernment. For what he saw in me on that day in 1984 was more than I knew of myself. My starting point had been to dress like a clown in order that I could more effectively hand out bits of paper to passersby in the street. Philip saw through that, to the clown I might become, made in the image of God.

A Challenging Place

In due course I got my invitation, filled in the tear-off slip, and sent it away. It seemed a good idea at that stage of the planning, but I distinctly remember that by the week of the event, I was afflicted with serious worries on two accounts. For a start, I hadn't heard anything from the person taking the bookings, and in addition I found myself struggling with a feeling that is familiar to all mothers: could I really leave my eighteen-month-old baby, Alethea, in the safe keeping of her dad and brothers Andrew and Mark? Of course, I knew she would be perfectly fine, and the problem was really mine: after all I had been through, would I be able to handle the separation not only from my child but also from the safety of the familiar territory of my home? People who know me today find it difficult to associate me with such feelings of insecurity, as I look to be so self-confident in all aspects of my ministry. I have to admit that my boldness sometimes surprises even myself, especially when speaking at large international conferences, and the difference between who I was then and who I am today is itself a testimony to the healing potential of clowning, not to mention the empowering work of God's Spirit.

But back to the training event, for the second problem came when I phoned to check up on my booking—they didn't seem to have it. Perhaps this was my moment to back out gracefully—and I said so. But the organizers were having none of it, and insisted that I was to be there and they would fit me in.

As the day arrived, I realized that the venue was not going to be the easiest place in the world to reach by public transport. To get there, I would have a journey by train and bus, followed by a fairly long walk around the outskirts of isolated parkland—and, since it was coming up on midwinter, it would be dark. I was scared, but having dealt with all my initial fears, I didn't want to plague my family with yet something else. However, we'd been married long enough for John easily to pick up all the telltale signs that I was having second thoughts about the venture, and he suggested taking me by car, which would make things much easier.

So I found myself on a dark Friday evening deposited outside a forbidding-looking church in a seedy part of Edinburgh, with my husband and kids eager to turn the car round to go back home, and urging me to go in! Once over the threshold, I found a very disparate bunch of people—though as a group they were wonderfully welcoming. The venue was like many churches in Scotland—a dingy hall furnished with carpets that had clearly seen better days and an assortment of clapped-out armchairs for us to sit in. Philip was his usual laid-back self—thank God—and the evening passed very quickly and painlessly, even though everyone else seemed much more confident than I felt able to be.

After we spent some time chatting and getting to know one another, we had a bit of an introduction to Christian clowning, and then a really old 16mm film projector was produced and precariously balanced on a wooden board, which in turn rested on top of a rickety coffee table. As the wheels of the old projector crunched on, it reminded me of the home movies my uncle James used to show to the family in the days of my Glasgow childhood. My favorite then had been a film called Stop Thief, a silent slapstick comedy in which a clown was chased through the streets and back gardens of a big city, bumping into people, colliding with dustbins and generally creating mayhem, while all the time being pursued by a burly police officer. He always found sanctuary inside a long shirt on a washing line, where he would be unnoticed by the police officer, who would run past without registering such an absurd sight. As I sat cross-legged on the floor watching with my cousin, she would be moved with pity for the poor man while I generally rolled about, helplessly laughing. Perhaps there had always been a clown dormant within me, and this was one of the things that Philip had recognized and that was about to be stirred into life.

Parable

Back in the clown workshop, we settled down to watch a film that I later discovered was *Parable:* the story of a man who dared to be different. The showing of it encapsulated all the worst features of a film show in a church: not only did the projector creak and groan the whole time, but there was no proper screen and Philip had to try to show it on to the wall—which in itself was easier said than done, as the place was falling to pieces, and he had to move the projector around several times before eventually finding a bit of wall that was not disfigured by peeling paint or bulging plaster. On top of all that, the copy of the film was of a very poor quality, and I really had to concentrate very hard indeed to peer at the scratched images emanating from the projector. But this collection of inauspicious circumstances only serves to underline how powerfully the images spoke to me, because the impact they made has never left me. From the moment I saw that film, I was absolutely captivated.

The film itself was produced by Fred A. Niles for the Protestant Council of the City of New York, where it formed the centerpiece of one of the exhibits at the 1964 New York World's Fair. The introductory words set the scene:

In the Gospels, Jesus teaches us by using parables. Through them comes God's message in simple story form. Today, a parable might begin like this: Once there was a great circus. In the march of nations and peoples, a great circus parade in which some were participants, some merely spectators. A parade in which human beings seldom knew one another, or cared for one another. And into this great circus of life came a man—who dared to be different . . .

After this introduction—which is spoken over a dark screen—the circus parade is shown in all its splendor and color. Elaborately carved coaches and carriages driven by liveried characters march down the highway accompanied by elephants, horses, llamas and all the other characters of the traditional circus. This is Circus Magnus, and in one early shot we see Magnus, the owner and ringmaster, a weary figure looking at his face in the mirror, wondering who he is and why he lives this way. Finally, just as the end of the procession disappears around a bend in the road, a camera shot looking backwards shows another person, clad entirely in white, with a white face bearing only the characteristic black marks of the cross over his eyes and riding on an understated little animal, a grey donkey. They plod along together always just out of sight, but keeping up with the rest of the procession.

Once the circus settles into its new performing site, there are lots of jobs to be done. The elephant trainer goes off to find a lake and fills heavy buckets of water for his animals who are now very thirsty after their long trek in the heat. He has to scramble down a steep bank with large buckets. Once filled, of course, they are much harder to deal with, and as he struggles up again there is the sort of classic clown gag that is so absurdly obvious that even the smallest child will get a laugh at it, as the elephant keeper puts his heavy burden down, turns around and transfers the two identical buckets into opposite hands. Struggling on, he takes a well-earned rest under a tree, leaving the buckets a couple of paces behind. In the distance the white-clad character spots him, approaches silently and then, after a pause, looks at him with affection before picking the buckets up and striding through the undergrowth towards the site. Realizing that his buckets have gone, the trainer jumps up and scrambles and stumbles to catch the "thief," only to discover him already giving the water to the first elephant as he arrives. By the time he checks that number one is all right and moves to number two, the water thief is just too far away to apprehend, though the trainer is so surprised at such helpful behavior that he leaves his elephants and follows after him at a distance.

Meanwhile, down at the fairground, a rough-looking man is throwing hard baseballs at a young African who is suspended on a ducking seat above a huge tank of water. If a ball hits the target above his head, the boy will automatically be dumped into the water. Can you guess who's watching from the sidelines? Of course—the character in white, who changes places with the boy and (predictably) ends up being ducked. But the boy returns to help him out—and the elephant trainer is still hanging around too. Meanwhile, the owner of the attraction is mad at them all and fills his pockets with ammunition before setting off in hot pursuit.

Inside another tent is a sideshow that involves a smart-looking character who forces a circus girl into a box while he apparently slices her into shreds by pushing sharp knives through from side to side. When the box opens, the man in white who had been watching sadly has changed places with her and they are laughing together as they run off. The circus organizers, however, are not amused at all.

The central scene of the film is the most graphic of all. It is shot inside the big top, with people sitting on those red-painted planks of wood often found at travelling circuses—easy to assemble and very uncomfortable to sit on, but at least they give everyone the same view. The audience is full of eager children who gaze as three characters are strapped into harnesses and then raised on ropes to the apex of the tent. This is the high point of the circus program: Magnus the Great and his Living Marionettes. They are, of course, a version of Punch and Judy, in which the characters are played by real people portrayed as puppets, and who are controlled by the vicious-looking Magnus who sits on a kind of throne, pulling their strings to make them do his bidding. As in the puppet version, Judy has her baby, who is battered in a very realistic way. There is a tangible, uneasy silence in the tent while this act goes on, and the children who are watching are clearly not enjoying it, especially when the baby is dropped from a great height.

Into this scene comes the character in white, who produces a feather duster and playfully starts cleaning the shoes of the children who are sitting with their feet perched on the first strut of wood. They laugh and start to tap their feet, and soon everyone wants their toes to be dusted. The elephant trainer, the African boy and the woman have by now become increasingly fascinated by this new personality who has made a difference to their lives, and they join in the fun. Predictably, Magnus—who should now be the main attraction—is definitely not pleased. But there is more to come, as the character in white moves over to the center of the ring and unfastens the ropes that hold up the puppets, lowering them carefully before he and his three new friends release the "living marionettes" from their imprisoning braces and set them free.

By now, the crowd are apprehensive about what will happen next and are pushing to get away from this rather anxious scene. As the braces dangle from the trapeze, the figure in white goes and fastens himself into them, whereupon Magnus the Great— who by now is seriously angry—points his whip at two willing accomplices and directs them to raise the character to the highest point in the tent. Ironically, they turn out to be the very individuals who themselves had been strung up only a short while before in their roles as Punch and the hangman.

As the white clown is lifted up, the man from the first sideshow pelts him with the baseballs he still has in his pocket. The fellow who had been ushering people into the big top with his walking-stick now uses it to strike the ascending figure, willingly assisted in this by the man with the swords from the magic trick. The clown puppet's arms and legs are pulled by the strings in all directions and it is clear that he has no control over the situation at all. As he lets out a bloodcurdling scream that resounds over the whole site, the camera takes a shot over the landscape outside as the sky turns dark. Magnus is both fascinated and disturbed by this strange individual who has spoiled his act. But the limp figure now hanging before him frustrates him even more than he did when alive, and he goes frantic with the strings, pulling them this way and that and all the while tossing the torpid figure in what seems like all directions at once. The final scene inside the tent shows the white clown strung up in the apex, arms spread wide by the strings that imprison him, and with the crossbeam of the trapeze gantry behind him. The entire circus site is silent.

By way of contrast, only a short distance away among the trees is a scene of peace and harmony. Sitting on the grass, the elephant trainer is undergoing an everyday transformation with a difference, shaving with a razor and an abundance of lather. The woman from the box of swords is holding a mirror for him to see his reflection, while behind him the boy from the ducking booth is kneeling down, offering him his own towel to dry his face. In the middle distance, the rest of the circus has already packed up and is moving on to the next venue. As at the beginning, Magnus the Great sits in his van being transported in grand style, as befits the owner of it all. In the final glimpse of him, he is looking again in his mirror and hesitatingly wondering if white makeup would make a difference to him too. Could there be the possibility of change even for this desperate character?

The answer is not spelled out in the film; only the questions are there. Did Magnus really change? Did the ducking boy, the elephant trainer and the woman take their freedom and find new direction permanently? The one thing that is certain at the end is that, as the circus rounds the bend in the road taking it away from this site, the guy in white is still there, straddling his donkey and following at a distance, watching out for those who need him most.

Today, *Parable* is available in an enhanced color version on video, so that a lot more of it is accessible than when I first saw it.[7] I use it often in teaching classes. But for me nothing—absolutely nothing—will ever have the impact of the scratchy black-and-white version that arrested me that night in such an inauspicious venue in a run-down part of Edinburgh. It must have been the nearest thing I've known to a Damascus road experience. This was the whole gospel from start to finish—abuse, suffering and violence of a fallen world, transformed by Jesus's love, humility and ultimate sacrifice—all condensed into a single day in the life and death of a circus clown. Jesus just leapt out of the picture—always there—compassion his driving force as he rescued those who were experiencing exploitation in whatever shape or form it came. He was constantly challenging the way things were being done, how people were treated, and just kept jumping up, particularly where human relationships were dysfunctional and people were ripping off others for their own advantage. Here was a Jesus who was not far from anyone who reached out to him, who was taking the flak even to the point of death—but most powerfully of all, through to resurrection. They simply could not destroy him, and there he was right at the end still following on his donkey and always ready to respond—but never pushing his way in uninvited, and even with a sense of humor.

Remember, this was all at a time when I was still struggling with the loss of my daughter, and as I watched, I realized that I had come face-to-face with the One who could make a difference. This was good news indeed, for the familiar pictures that I knew from scripture were right here for me—and that was reassuring—but dressed in clothing (both metaphorically and literally) that I found both mind-blowing and exhilarating. I just knew that in some way beyond my understanding, this was for me.

Steps in New Directions

After that first evening we were all introduced to our hosts. I was taken home by a lovely family who had not known they were having me until they had foolishly volunteered the fact that they could unexpectedly put up an extra one. "Up" was the right word: their six-year-old son was staying away for the weekend, and that was why they had space for me. His bed was literally on top of his wardrobe—a particular sort of design well suited to small boys in order to maximize space. I climbed up the ladder and got into bed, though I immediately realized that I am a bit bigger than a six-year-old! I spent most of that night reading magazines that I had taken "just in case" I couldn't sleep or found myself at a loose end for some reason. At least it ensured I had no trouble being up for the next session bright and early, even though it was a Saturday morning. I headed off to the hall to find I wasn't the first to arrive. A funny little guy who cracked jokes all the time was there already, though I remember trying to figure out how he'd made it in time, as I felt sure that the night before he had left to catch a train back to Glasgow (the other side of the country). I later discovered that this was Tommy Thomson, another person who had gone to that weekend looking for new directions for his life, and who later emerged as a totally different style of clown from either Valentine or Barni. He became (and is) Clownbo, specializing in balloon modeling and street work, and is now a member of the group of Celtic Christian Clowns mentioned in chapter 4.

I remember one of the leaders on this day inviting us to jump between two chairs, land, balance, be consciously aware of who we were, and then to say in our preferred way, "I am . . ." It was an incredibly difficult exercise—more difficult for some of us than for others. I remember thinking that it would have been so much easier for me to be at home, even though I might have been cleaning, shopping, visiting the swing park, having fun with the kids and cooking the lunch all at the same time—though, since it was Saturday, I probably should have been enjoying a morning off anyway. I realized that one of the ways I had been dealing with my personal tragedy was by making myself very busy. It is a comparatively easy thing to do, and I suspect that most of us find ourselves in this kind of situation at some time or other. If we are busy, we have no time to reflect on who we are, let alone about who we might be in the process of becoming. I think that at that point in my life, not only was I suffering, but I was supremely shy about either exploring or reflecting on who I might be. Of course, I could have a conversation with anyone—but who was I, really? Believe it or not, addressing that question was one of the hardest things I had to do. Maybe it sounds silly, but it sums up where clowns often find themselves. In the game, we all had the opportunity to break out of the circle, where we had the support of others, and step into the middle—not to show off, but rather the opposite, to become vulnerable. That, for me, is the secret of successful clown ministry. It is a neat balancing act between personal security and enormous weakness. When you are out there on your own, you can never hide behind someone else, which is why I am always vulnerable; but if you haven't already found your source of personal strength before that point, you are likely to fold up and die.

Later in the morning I had the opportunity, with the others, to experiment with makeup. This is yet another whole process of discovery in itself. For a start, there is a decision to be made about what kind of makeup to use. Am I going to be a white face (all white plus the colors on top)? Could I be an Auguste (the character usually with flesh-tone skin but large white patches for the eyes and big red mouth, outlined in black)? Or might I be a tramp or hobo clown? As we played with the makeup, different people made their own choices, and there must have been some of each type. I decided to go for all white to start with. Though most women wear makeup frequently, it's not usually stark white. The first thing the white does is to give a blank sheet on which to paint. So I had my new start. Then it was time to have fun with the colors of life. I needed to do this a few times and allow myself to make changes.

Once I got the feel for it, I realized that what made the difference wasn't the amount of paint I used, but how I used it. I had to take a good look at myself first, because a clown character face is really a cartoon of the person. Understanding that in itself can be an invaluable part of the process of self-discovery, looking at and understanding who we are and then, like a cartoonist, exaggerating it so other people can see it more clearly. Tommy Thomson knew who he was right away, and created an Auguste character for himself.

When we were all ready, we went for a "Plunge"—the occasion when a new clown goes out into the street for the first time. Philip Noble had already discovered that one or two of us could do little bits of juggling, and we could all sing and play fun instruments. So, with just a little encouragement from him, we formed a troupe to walk out in the street to the nearby shopping precinct. Before we left, we'd been reminded of the need to support one another. So off we went—and I was thinking that since these weren't my local shops, at least I wouldn't meet anybody I knew. We learned very quickly that once in the street as a clown, people want to talk, want to shake hands, and generally interact. I remember going to a traditional cafe with lace curtains halfway up the front window, and peeping over the curtains—at which some middle-aged women hooted with laughter and started waving back to me. Normally if I had looked through a cafe window in Edinburgh, I would have got a very different response, either being ignored completely or told to move on. As a group, we juggled and played, and when anyone dropped a prop we remembered to give an exaggerated "Ahhhh . . ." of sympathy, with appropriate accompanying gestures. Equally, when they did well, we all clapped enthusiastically. We sang and shook hands with everyone, gave away some balloons, before finally making our way back to the church hall.

I'm tempted to say that we had a strong cup of coffee to calm our shaking nerves. I think we did have coffee, but actually we were all on a high to start with. We'd only been out for quite a short time, but as we unpacked what we had learned, one discovery stood out above all the others, and that was the importance of teamwork. When you drop something while juggling, if people empathize with you and help you to get going again you are given confidence to try it again. If no help had been given, it would have been very easy to slink off home. I unconsciously thought of the many churches, communities and families I knew where supportive teamwork and mutual affirmation could transform their corporate life. Furthermore, I realized we had all learned that lesson in a powerful way that would be hard for us to forget—and in such a short time. This was worth pondering on, as also was the ease with which the general public had wanted to engage with us. We had been welcomed into their Saturday afternoon outings. We had not pushed our way in. Of course, we were open to rejection—but it didn't happen.

This being a church-based workshop, part of the expectation was that the group would be responsible for a service the next day. So after coffee, we practiced how we might present a song in a clown sort of way as part of the service on the Sunday morning. After more exploration of new clown skills, we all went home to have supper with our various host families. As he'd done the night before, Tommy rushed off—though once more he was back in good time on the Sunday morning. It was only years later, when we met up again, that we realized we must be "clown twins," for Valentine and Clownbo both finally came to birth that week-end—and I discovered that Tommy worked for the train company and had a free travel pass, which is why he had gone back and forth between Edinburgh and Glasgow each day. He must have had about as little sleep as I had.

I don't recall much about the service, except that we all took part in it. Philip led, wearing a distinctive alb that made him look like a medieval monk, and I overheard a child sitting near me ask, "Is that what a clown looks like?" I've often wondered if she got a satisfactory answer—and her question raised all sorts of mischievous thoughts in my mind about some of the strange things we wear and do in church. The congregation usually had lunch together as part of their regular community life, and after sharing with them we reluctantly said our farewells and I caught the train back home. It was so good to see my family again, and get back to my normal routine. But would I ever be able to describe myself as normal again? And what would "normal" look like from now on?

Space to Explore Something New

The sense of excitement I felt and the new insights I had shared that weekend were received less than enthusiastically in my own church. They did what all Christians do when they don't want to know about something: they just ignored it, and hoped that the subject would go away. In a significant way, that is exactly what did happen. One thing I have learned is not to be pushy about sharing anything in church. Jesus never pushed his way into places where he was not welcome, and when he sent seventy of his followers out he advised them not to waste time with people who were not open to their message (Luke 10:1-12). Looking back, I suppose I had secretly hoped that my church would have responded positively to my finding a new direction in life and ministry, but their apathy had at least one positive benefit, for it encouraged me to reflect on all that had happened to me, and what I thought I had learned, without feeling pressurized into doing something publicly with it all immediately. Though I would still have valued some support and affirmation, I can see with the benefit of hindsight that having that personal reflection space played a big part in the direction I would subsequently take.

As a matter of fact, the alienation and resistance I encountered from within the church community at that time was significantly instrumental in helping me to discover the kind of clown minister I would become. During this period of enforced reflection, I was given a copy of *The Clown Ministry Handbook* by Janet Litherland.[8] I found this to be an invaluable book, not least because it was written in a way that enabled me to dip into it and reflect on small sections before going back to another part for more inspiration. At one point she says, "There is more to becoming a clown than makeup, wardrobe and a few tricks. Not even a course in clowning ensures a true clown. (S)he develops from within, from an inner warmth and an intense desire to give pleasure, to make whole persons out of broken bits and pieces. Does this sound like ministry?" I knew that it did for me—not only as a way to follow, but as something that rang true to my own experience. I had been broken into small bits and pieces, and had experienced God lovingly putting me back together again. As I thought about these concepts, they were articulating something I had already explored in a different medium through my own traumatic experiences of pain.

Janet Litherland goes on to add that "clown ministry isn't just entertainment; nor is it preaching in costume. It is a means of touching souls, something most clowns somehow manage to do. Perhaps all clowns, whether or not they realize it, are involved in ministry." This also expressed a biblical concept which had gradually been growing in significance for me, that as human beings we are all made in the image of God (Genesis 1:26-27). This is the reason we often recognize Christlike characteristics in people who would not claim to be Christian, and as I thought more deeply about it, this seemed a very good way of understanding ministry—as a desire to see the broken and not-so-broken becoming whole people, renewed and reflecting God's image.

As I read further, I became aware of the fact that what was happening to me was also happening on a bigger stage around the world, and that in many countries there was a great rediscovery of the place of the arts in relation not only to worship, but also to theology. Though I already knew a good deal about the history of Western Christianity, I began to appreciate it from a different angle. The received wisdom, at least in the circles in which I had moved up to that time, had been very positive about the emergence in Scotland of a word-based expression of faith, in which God spoke largely through sermons, and church buildings were stripped of anything that might be considered a distraction to those who were either listening to sermons or preaching them. Without drawing a false antithesis between thinking and feeling, I came to see just how impoverished much worship had become as a result of the post-Reformation marginalization of the gifts of human creativity. If creativity was actually the first of God's own attributes (and it does appear on the very first page of the Bible), what might this be saying to today's church? Perhaps this was a time for us to begin to dig further back in history than we have often done, and rediscover the most ancient roots of the faith.

Floyd Shaffer was another author who influenced me at this period. He is a Lutheran pastor working in America, and in the late 1960s he started thinking about the possible use of clowning in ministry. Indeed, he is widely credited with having been the person who brought to birth the concept of clowning as ministry, certainly in the USA. I was intrigued with the way in which he transposed the whole liturgy into a clowning celebration that he carries through totally in silent mime. When my Barni character came to birth many years later, Floyd Shaffer's example was to become the inspiration for the way I presented Barni's silent communion, and then developed a fresh style of verbal reflections on the meaning of it all. One of the things that particularly impressed me about his work and writing was the way he emphasized the importance of integrating clowning with other experiences in people's lives in a way that could happen only through the work of God's Spirit. He includes a story to illustrate this:

> In a clown worship in Colorado, I had accidentally put too much flash and smoke powder in my flashpot. When it went off, the church was engulfed in blue smoke. People coughed good-naturedly. The smoky experience was followed by the discovery of bread and wine for communion.
> Afterward, a man approached me and said, "The most wonderful thing about the service was the flashpot." He then told me he had been in Korea. A shell had exploded, killing all his buddies, and he had been covered with their blood. This clown service was the first time he had smelt something like that Korean battle. As he smelled the smoke, he put it all together, "In the midst of hell, Jesus Christ is with me."[9]

The idea of bread and wine appearing after a flash of smoke may surprise you. I have certainly never actually seen this done, although I would be interested to do so. However, it is impossible to read this and fail to see that the man's deep need had been addressed, and presumably nothing else had touched his spirit in quite this way before. I can understand something of this phenomenon when I look back to leading a Good Friday service with John in St Andrews Episcopal Church in the city of St Andrews, Scotland. The service lasted for three hours, and was split into half-hour sections, which allowed people freedom to stay for the whole thing or come and go if they wished. Because that year (1995) was the fiftieth anniversary of the execution of Dietrich Bonhoeffer, we decided to use distinctive phrases from his writings as the themes of each section: "To obey is to believe"; "A world come of age"; "God at the center of life"; "Religionless Christianity"; "Cheap and costly grace"; and "Christ existing as community." Each of the thirty-minute segments had its own unique visual representation. Under "God at the center of life," John told the story of The Ragman[10] and then Barni produced the elements of bread and wine, barbed wire, cross and nails from gleanings of rubbish collected from waste bins. Under "Religionless Christianity," a tree and nails was used as a focus for personal prayer, as I have described earlier in chapter 5. In "A world come of age," after some visual representations depicting sexual abuse and domestic violence, and during the singing of John Bell's chant "Behold the Lamb of God,"[11] the congregation was invited to light candles, which were then placed in the chancel in the shape of a giant cross to represent victims of abuse known to them and for whom they wanted to pray.

Since this was Scotland, I took my time introducing all this. I had my back to the congregation, so I had no idea if anyone at all would move out of their seats. It was always possible they would find it too embarrassing. So with measured movements I lit my candle and placed it in the heart of the cross in the sand, and as I turned to pray I was staggered to see that there was a line of people queuing up to the end of that huge building, and more joining as space became available. That in itself was quite moving, but what was even more astonishing was a phone call I had a couple of weeks later. It was from a man who had been able to arrive only for the later parts of the service. In planning it this way, it had never occurred to us to take account of the impact of several hundred candles burning for two or three hours, and those who had been there from the start thought nothing of it either. But to this individual arriving late, the first thing that hit him was a huge pall of smoke rising from the heart of the church and billowing up into the lofty heights of the central tower. He was profoundly moved just by that, as it reminded him of the experience of the prophet Isaiah (Isaiah 6:1-8, a story with which he was familiar). In that story, Isaiah was caught up through the smoke in the temple to a fresh encounter with God which ended with him being sent on his mission, and that was exactly what had happened to this person. As he shared this, he kept impressing on me that he was a university psychologist and should have known how to deal with such sensory experiences. What had taken place wasn't supposed to happen to people like him. Perhaps not, by the laws of rationality alone, but when the Spirit of God gets to work then anything can happen, and often does.

There is a sense of continuity between Floyd Shaffer's story and this one, which again ought not to be too surprising, for when similar things begin to happen in different forms of ministry and in different places, that is one of the signs that God is truly at work. I recognize so often in my clowning that I can go only so far with people, and then I need to give them space to continue alone, which can often be space for God to do that special work with them. It's important to know when to step back and not intrude. One of the reasons it's so beneficial to be Barni is that it's completely true to character for a hobo to slip away unnoticed.

Touching the Whole of Life

When I first started clowning, I wore a bright yellow shirt and shoes and blue dungarees with yellow stripes, decorated with some beads in bright blue and yellow. The only thing that really made it a clown's outfit was my multicolored wig and face makeup. Otherwise, these were fashionable clothes that I could easily use for everyday wear. One day I set off dressed this way (minus the wig and paint) to take the children to school and go shopping. In the afternoon I made a chaplaincy visit to a women's prison, and then, after picking the children up from school and cooking the meal, I went off to take a clown event in a church with some young people. I had been in the same clothes all day, and had only added the wig and face paints for the evening event. Reflecting on that, I realized that clowning had become an integral part of my life. Whether looking after my children and doing the most ordinary of jobs, or ministering to prisoners or working in church with teenagers, the whole of my life as a Christian ought to be marked by the values of the kingdom of God. I can't behave one way at home and another way outside (though in reality, many of us behave worst with the people we know best). To have integrity, my life has to mirror these values at all times. I felt that in some small way, having done such a variety of things in one day, dressed in the same gear, had underlined this for me.

I find that this is the kind of process from which I often learn the most. Things happen, and then as I unpack them and reflect on them I begin to understand them. I remember meeting Peruvian theologian Gustavo Gutiérrez, one of the founders of the liberation theology movement, and being encouraged when he told me that his experience had begun with following Jesus, and theological reflection had followed from that—discipleship being the first act, and theology the second. The more I reflect back on my personal spiritual journey intertwined with my clowning, the more I understand. Reflection time doesn't happen easily in busy lives. We need to be intentional about giving ourselves that sacred space. I have already referred in a previous chapter to something I learned from Danish theologian Søren Kierkegaard, but his wisdom is worth repeating here, that "We live life forwards and reflect backwards." Part of the difficulty we live with today is that we don't give ourselves enough time to reflect.

Chapter 9

Theological Reflections

Doing Theology

Mention of theology can be a real turnoff for creative people. Those of you who are theologically trained will already have recognized that my way of doing theology is essentially an inductive approach, trying things out first, exploring stories of how God works in people's lives, and then allowing the theology to emerge out of subsequent reflection on all that. This is fundamentally different from the deductive approach that has dominated the scene up until now, where theology was believed to consist of a series of rational truths that followed from universally established first principles just as surely as night follows day. It is now coming to be recognized that "truth," whatever it may be, is more appropriately understood not as a collection of static propositions, but as something lively and living—a concept that is especially appropriate in the context of a faith whose founder claimed that "I am . . . the truth" (John 14:6), thereby placing "truth" very firmly in the context of interpersonal relationships rather than leaving it imprisoned in abstractions.

There is, of course, a valid place for analytical reflection, but there are many good reasons for believing that the kind of dynamic interplay between action and reflection that I see as central to clown ministry is actually the way that Christian theology is supposed to be done. It is what Jesus did, and it has played a major part in the massive growth of the Church throughout the non-Western world in the second half of the 20th century. Moreover, there are signs that even the traditional theological establishment in the West is waking up to realize that our inherited models, inspired most immediately by the values of the Enlightenment, and further back still by the rationality of the ancient Greeks, do not represent the only ways of doing things, and probably are not the most useful ones at this point in our cultural development. In his ground-breaking book *A Fundamental Practical Theology*, Don S. Browning has reminded us "that practical thinking is the center of human thinking and that theoretical and technical thinking are abstractions from practical thinking. If one takes this seriously and relates it to theology, it fundamentally changes the historic formulations of the organization of the theological disciplines. It is a revolution long overdue."[12] As I reflect on my own work from this wider perspective, I see my clown ministry, and indeed this book, as both a product of and a contribution to that revolution. So I am going to continue sharing more stories as a way of exploring some of the theological implications of clowning in a Christian context.

Maybe some of you are wondering how I could have called this chapter "theological reflection," because most of us imagine that that sort of thing has to be expressed in verbose language overloaded with abstract cognitive ideas. If you look for them, you will easily find some things that almost fit that description. But I have deliberately included a lot of stories, because they are central to the kind of theology that emerges from the experience of Christian clowning, and on which in turn clown ministry is based. There has been a strong emphasis on weakness, on finding God through vulnerability and in the small things of life. This too is central to clown theology. But more than that, it is central to the biblical witness about the Gospel itself being "foolishness" and the messengers of God themselves being the little people of this world, who are of no consequence to those obsessed with power and their own self-opinionated wisdom (1 Corinthians 1:18-31). It is also central to what is happening in the growing churches of today's world. This is theology from the bottom up, theology as it is encountered and articulated by the disinherited, by the abused and by the marginalized—theology as it is supposed to be when the values of God's kingdom are what drive us forward in the belief that with God's help the weak can become strong and the powerless can be empowered. And it all starts with taking seriously the Christian doctrines of creation and incarnation, and in that light being open to see the world the way God sees it, through the cross.

One of the major events I have spoken at in recent years was the Anglican Conference on Evangelism, organized by the Church of England Board of Mission in early 1999 to mark the end of the worldwide Decade of Evangelism, and one of the themes I wanted to look at in my sessions there was the nature of vulnerability. The conference was a week-long event, and once I had settled into my room I went to join the others who were gathering for afternoon tea. As often happens at such events, many people seemed to know one another and were busy looking out for and greeting old friends. Though I knew a lot of the participants myself, I couldn't at that point see anyone I recognized, and so as I collected my cup of tea and scone I was surveying the assembled crowd, looking for someone who might welcome being engaged in conversation by a stranger. I don't like announcing to people that I'm the speaker. For one thing, it's generally more illuminating to remain unidentified for as long as possible: it gives you a better feel of what's going on, and also people don't seem to have the same need to impress if you don't appear to be anybody in particular. Of course, I knew that one of the first questions I would be asked would be which diocese I was representing, and that would probably mean I would have to come clean and admit why I was there.

As I looked around, my attention was almost immediately attracted to one person who, unlike all the others, was not drinking tea. She was drinking from her mother's breast, was only four months old, and was called Naomi. So I started to make friends with Naomi and her mother. By the end of the week she had turned out to be my very best ally in addressing the question of vulnerability, because her mother generously allowed me to take her on to the platform on the last day in order to serve as a living—and lively—visual image to help me introduce the subject. There were about four hundred delegates there, and when I asked who had met Naomi over the course of the previous days, the vast majority raised their hands. If there had been a competition to see who had personally connected with the largest number of strangers, she would easily have won the prize. I started to talk about vulnerability, in particular how God's personal nature had been shown to us most profoundly by God choosing, in the person of Jesus, to become a child. I reminded them how, when Jesus wanted to set out a model of true discipleship, he chose a child as the example we should follow, rather than one of the great and the good (of whom there had been no shortage at that particular conference). At that, quite spontaneously Naomi yawned down my microphone and the delegates erupted in laughter. Not for the first time did I reflect on how laughter can be such an effective learning experience—though the real teacher of course was not me, but the child who was at that stage unable to speak, and who could do nothing but lie in my arms, totally vulnerable, trusting me. Naomi clearly communicated a great deal more in that one yawn than I did with all my additional explanations.

The significance of this was not lost on others who were there. For who is more vulnerable than a baby? A baby is totally dependent for all her needs on another caring person, most commonly her mother. She can't feed or look after herself, and the most she can do is intimate that she needs help—something babies usually do quite effectively. At the heart of the gospel is the extraordinary claim that God became a child, and chose to take on human flesh, to be like us. In other words, God became vulnerable. God as a human in the form of Jesus could be received or rejected, cared for or abused, nurtured or stifled, loved or hated. This is the way Jesus came into our world and this is also the way he sends us. At the end of the fourth Gospel he says, in what are almost his final words to the disciples, "As the Father has sent me, so send I you" (John 20:21-23). The subtext is that, sent in the way Jesus was, we as his followers might be received, though on the other hand we might easily be rejected; we might be cared for, but equally we may be abused; we may be welcomed with open arms and loved, or just as readily we might be hated.

A Christian clown can be a living picture of all this. Since Jesus is the Christian clown's model, it is important for me to have continuity with his behavior and for my message to have integrity with his. Of course, this should always be the case whether I am in clown costume or not. But in relation to clowning, it means that I always need first to affirm other people. This was the way in which Jesus consistently operated. A classic example—though by no means the only one—is the story of the woman of Samaria whom Jesus met at the well (John 4:7-30). From the viewpoint of conventional religion, she had many things wrong with her and was the last kind of person who could have expected affirmation from those who were somebody. Even Jesus's own disciples (who were themselves nobodies) were surprised that he should have been having dealings with her. From their perspective, everything about her seemed to be wrong, from her ethnic origins to her personal lifestyle.

But Jesus operated on a different level of perception altogether. Instead of ridiculing or rejecting her, he valued her as a person made in God's image, and therefore of infinite worth. By admitting to her that he himself was thirsty, he placed himself in a weak position, for she could easily have ignored his need for water. In reality, she was so impressed by his personal vulnerability and his willingness to see her as a person of value that as their conversation unfolded it was the most natural thing in the world for her to react positively to Jesus's invitation to move on to explore new possibilities and different ways of being.

Translated into clowning terms, this is expressed in the themes already explored through our discussion of the film *Parable* in chapter 8. Expressed more prosaically, I'm the one who needs to receive the custard pie rather than throwing it at others—or, more imaginatively perhaps, if I throw one I need to ensure it will miss the target and come back to my own face instead.

Authentic Ways of Being

I remember, quite early in my clowning ministry, calling Philip Noble after a particular event where someone had been especially rude to me. I was feeling quite sorry for myself and in need of someone to commiserate with. He very wisely counselled, "And what did you expect? What happened to Jesus? If you are his follower, why should you expect anything different?"

Actually, it is very rare indeed for me to get a negative response to my clowning, but all Christians should remember that they are sent in the same way as Jesus. Historically, the church in the West has often preferred to adopt a somewhat triumphalist attitude rather than the model of vulnerability presented by Jesus. No doubt this owes a lot to the imperialist enterprises of our forebears, and the way in which the whole of life in previous centuries was dominated by the concerns of warfare. It was easy—even natural—for military imagery to be applied to the life and witness of the church. For many men in particular, their entire worldview was determined by what they either witnessed or heard of on the battlefield, something that inevitably gave them a predisposition to using analogies of death to articulate biblical values. As a result, the ways in which Christian theology was expressed tended to focus on matters such as guilt, accountability and judgment, with a corresponding diminution of the kind of images of new life and new possibilities to which Jesus more often bore witness. As a woman, I find that images of birth are a more appropriate way of expressing faith, focusing on nurture and facilitation and the expectation that we can all yet become what intrinsically we are, namely women and men together made in the image of God. The concept of personal transformation that undergirds that outlook is central to everything I do as a clown.

Some will no doubt dismiss all this as just a trendy notion that appeals to the mood of the moment. In reality, though, it is deeply rooted in the very first words of the entire Bible, which depict God as creator bringing forth humankind, women and men together as equals living and working in a spirit of mutuality. Since part of what it means to be made "in God's image" (Genesis 1:26) is that we are both called and empowered to share in God's own creativity, then if we are to reflect a true picture of who God is to our own culture, we too need to be working together in a spirit of mutuality—something that is embodied not only in what God created but also in the relational way in which God did it ("Let us make humankind . . . ").

Of course, women will not put things right by copying the kind of mistakes that men have already made. We need to discover new ways to work together in harmony. Whether or not that makes me a feminist, I will leave other people to judge. But it certainly disturbs me when I meet women in the Church who are unconcerned about such matters. For Christians to imagine that this is not an important issue merely highlights the extent to which many church people have lost touch with the wider society in which they live. I do not understand why some Christian women will say to me, as some did not long ago, "But we don't mind at all being called 'sons of God.'" I suppose that people who can say that probably live in relationships where they feel so affirmed and cherished that this is not an issue for them—though even then I recognize that such a response is, at bottom, engendered by the deeply ingrained assumption that, in the Church if not in the rest of life, the power and control will ultimately rest with men who will exercise it in a macho, characteristically "male" sort of way. There is, however, a wider implication that should always challenge us here, because we are supposed to be bearing witness to—indeed establishing—the kingdom of God and kingdom values. Even for those who do not find themselves in an apparently oppressive situation, it should be of concern that others do find themselves in that quandary, and Christians are called to identify with the vulnerable and act in solidarity with them.

I remember being at a prestigious dinner at a British university where my husband and Sir Jonathon Porritt had been dialoguing on religion and matters of environmental concern. The remaining guests represented a broad cross-section of academic life, both women and men. In the course of conversation, the university vice-chancellor commented that he had recently received a delegation of female employees asking about some specific rights, and he was looking for ways to affirm their request. I can't remember the exact point at issue, but I do remember that the only people to make negative comments about the request that was made were a couple of female professors who declared that, so far as they were concerned, this was merely pandering to political correctness—something that was obviously not a good thing to do, in their opinion. Being "only a clown," I was scrambling around in my brains to think how I could challenge this line without being too provocative at what was, after all, a social occasion at which I was one of the main guests. In the event, Sir Jonathon himself allowed the two women to say their piece, and then, when they had eventually run out of steam, he gently drew attention to their education and privileged positions in society and pointed out that, for those very reasons, it was therefore their responsibility to take up the concerns of those less fortunate than themselves as though they were their own concerns.

Moving on to what looked like safer territory, they then asked me about my own work. Since they knew that I taught theology, I can still remember the look on their faces when I told them I am also a clown! I have to confess that I do really get quite a thrill out of telling people this, especially on pompous occasions when they are busy name-dropping and trying to score points off one another. I imagine it's the sort of thing Jesus did. He certainly did on at least one occasion, when the religious authorities were looking for his temple tax and he told Peter to go and catch a fish and pay with the coin it was holding in its mouth (Matthew 17:24-27)!

One of the other things I have learned over this period is the importance of the way we refer to God. For as long as I can remember, I have always used inclusive language of people (no "men" and "mankind" when I really meant everyone), but it was Raymond Fung who first drew my attention to the same issue in theological terms, when in a low key and non-confrontational manner he said to me that if I was going to teach worldwide I ought to think about grappling with God-language. Up to that point it simply hadn't crossed my mind, yet this was another lesson I had to learn from a culture that was not my own. I respected Raymond because his perspective had been forged by his experience of industrial mission in the sweatshops of Hong Kong. He knew firsthand of the situation of many victims, almost all of whom were women, and he had himself discovered that portraying a God who is exclusively male is unlikely to commend the gospel to many of today's people, not to mention the fact that it is also unfaithful to scripture.

I know well enough that God cannot be defined metaphysically or analytically, as it were, by reference to the interior components of the divine being, but only by analogy to persons and experiences with which we are familiar from other areas of human life. Within that frame of reference, God can of course be described as a Father, because the divine-human relationship can indeed be as close and life-giving as the best of human family ties. But God is also the Mother of her people, as evidenced by several biblical passages. An early piece of Hebrew poetry, the "Song of Moses," celebrates not only "the Rock, who fathered you" but also "the God who gave you birth" (Deuteronomy 32:18). Elsewhere, God is described crying out "like a woman in childbirth" (Isaiah 42:14), and showering her people with the affection of a mother (Isaiah 49:15, 66:13). What that can mean is highlighted by passages like Psalm 131:2, where God's love for people is compared with quiet rest in the arms of a divine mother, or Hosea 11:1-4 where God is pictured doing all the things for the people of Israel that a mother (rather than a father) would most naturally undertake. Jesus too uses female imagery to describe his own love for people (Matthew 23:37).

Once I became aware of the importance of all this, not only in relation to the concerns of today's women but also in relation to allowing the full breadth of scripture to inform my attitudes, I had no problem using inclusive language for God. When I started doing so, what did rather take me by surprise was the significant number of women who would come to me and express their appreciation of the fact that I was making the effort to take account of such matters.

At about the same time, I was writing a book on ministering to families, and in one chapter I had used the work I had been doing with families in the Scottish judicial system to illuminate aspects of the Abraham stories—something else that enabled me to see that to many children today, it is not good news to learn that God is like a father, or indeed any other male figure.[13]

Of course, with mime, this problem does not arise. But the whole debate does have a direct connection with Christian clowning because historically gender does not exist for the clown. A clown is seen as genderless and asexual, another feature of my characters that allows absolutely anyone to relate to my ministry. The realization that we are all either women or men made in the image of God has a power all its own, and is indeed good news to people who have a poor self-image. We first of all need to experience our own value and worth in God's eyes before we are ever going to communicate God's love to anyone else.

Carrying the Cross

When I tell my clown story I use many different starting points, depending on who the audience might be. But at the heart of the story there will always be the invitation that God gave to me, to begin to see the world the way God sees it. I regard this not only as intrinsic to my own story, but also as an authentic way to make a theological comment with integrity on every aspect of life. What does God see when looking at the world we inhabit? Warfare? Dysfunction in families? Social breakdown? Injustice? Wealth disproportionately spread? Disease? Death? Poisoned creation? It is through their power to deal with all these things, and many more, that the life, death and resurrection of Jesus continue to have relevance to life in the 21st century. Whenever God looks at our world it is always through the perspective of the cross, because that both acknowledges the reality of human suffering and highlights the opportunity for things to be made whole again.

I realized, as I shared this insight, that although many people knew this in a theoretical sort of way, seeing it presented visually as well as verbally by Valentine had the effect of making them sit up and want to do something about it. They needed the space to respond to what God was saying to them. With this awareness, I very tentatively started to invite people from my audiences to come and have the crosses painted on their own eyes, hands, or whatever, as a sign that they too wanted to begin to see the world the way God sees it. One of the first times I remember doing this was in Sydney in a very average suburban church, at a Sunday evening event. In the congregation were a young couple who came forward holding hands, and the way they looked at each other told everyone they were deeply in love. They asked to have crosses painted not on their eyes, but on their hands, "because," as they said, "we want as a couple who are committed to Jesus and also in love to touch each other in ways that are glorifying to God." Wow! That was as much a challenge for me as it was for them. I started to wonder how many churches give young people a safe space to face that particular question as they grow up.

On the day that Diana, Princess of Wales, died, I was in the Shetland Isles at the start of Bible Week, an ecumenical event held each year in the community. John and I were sharing the speaking at the various meetings that had been set up, and we had decided that I would be the one to give the address at the opening night. No one except us knew what we had planned, but between us we had agreed that I would share the story of Valentine and then we would invite people to have crosses painted on them as a sign that they wanted to "see the world the way God sees it."

Earlier that day, as we shared a meal with one of the local clergy, he warned us that Shetlanders are very private people and probably we shouldn't expect to be too adventurous. At an earlier stage in my ministry, I might easily have held back because of a statement like that. But by then I'd been doing it for long enough to realize that, quite often, the person with the real fear is the one who gives you the warning, and I shall for ever be glad that on that night, of all nights, I listened to the prompting of the inner voice and refused to be distracted from my intention to invite people to come and have the crosses painted. In no time at all, the space at the front of the church was crowded with people who wanted to respond, and many others were lining the aisles and prayerfully making their way from all parts of the church. Of course, all of those there had been affected in some way by the news of Diana's tragic death. But it was still a surprise for some that in such an apparently reserved community so many would respond. And their responses were by no means limited to the emotional concerns of that particular day. A minister (a man) came to me and said, "I've only been here three weeks and I need to see Shetland the way God sees it." Was he finding the adjustment hard? I don't know, but I'm sure God answered that prayer. A woman came to John, who was standing at the opposite side of the church to me, and said, "I need the cross painted right across my body." As he listened and prayed with her, and then applied the cross, she told a harrowing story of a life in which she had been a victim of abuse and needed deep healing from her suffering. Others asked for crosses to be painted on their hands and feet, in ways that related to the particular work they did.

Immediately before that, I had been in Wisconsin to speak at the annual Evangelism Conference of the American Baptist Churches of the USA. Probably one of the things that most attracted me to speak at this conference was its theme, "Coloring Outside the Lines." The relevance of painting with colors and giving people paint boxes struck a chord within me, as also did the question, "What happens when we scribble over the edges?"—something that I interpreted as taking risks like Jesus did. I was the keynote speaker on the very first evening, so I had no time to get the feel of the people or gauge the mood of the conference. On the contrary, I was aware that the mood of the week was probably going to be significantly determined by whatever I said to get it underway. So I was a bit apprehensive, and when I was only a few minutes into my talk and an African American guy at the back started jumping up and down, waving his arms at me and shouting, I wondered whatever I was supposed to do next. But I guess my underlying Scottish politeness took over and, without thinking, I asked him to repeat himself so that I could hear what he was saying. You can tell I have had no experience with hecklers! It didn't even occur to me to ignore him. But I soon worked out what was going on, when he intoned in an animated voice, "Preach on, sister!"—a sentiment that was loudly applauded by the rest of the audience. I had forgotten that this was the denomination in which Martin Luther King Jr had been a minister. Certainly, all my experience in Scottish churches had left me totally unprepared for such an affirming experience, though that didn't stop me from very quickly adapting to the interactive style of the occasion. Looking back, I don't think I have ever spoken anywhere in the world where I felt so encouraged as I did at that conference.

A few weeks later, I was leading worship for a conference of what was then called the Council of Churches for Britain and Ireland (now Churches Together in Britain and Ireland)—and John commented to me that I had been more affected by that time in Wisconsin than I knew, when I asked them why they weren't responding without apparently realizing that to do such a thing would have been totally out of character for British church leaders.

Before the opening service at Green Lake, Wisconsin, I had met with David Laubach, one of the organizers, and asked him about using the response with the crosses after I had spoken that night. He responded warmly but said he would run it past Brenda Halliburton, a petite woman whom I just loved from the moment I met her. It turned out that Brenda (an African American woman) was in charge of the event, and David (a male of European descent) was the assistant, and they worked together perfectly. As a matter of fact, that is one of the few groups I have worked with where men and women collaborated and supported one another in a totally unselfconscious way. It came so naturally to them, I don't think they realized how distinctive they would be in the wider Christian world. They simply did what they were each good at, and helped one another. When I commented on this, they drew my attention to the legacy of Martin Luther King Jr. and the civil rights movement, and I appreciated for the first time just how deeply the many different kinds of discrimination in the world are interconnected, and began to understand why those who have experienced abuse on the grounds of race and color often have such a high level of commitment to addressing and dealing with the question of gender, which for them was just another form of victimization.

That evening, many people came to have crosses painted on their person. The one that challenged me most was an African American pastor who came and rolled up his shirt to reveal his chest with huge scalpel wounds from the surgeon's knife. "I need God to heal me," he said simply. This was worship in a totally different dimension from what I more typically encounter, whether in the Reformed "hymn-prayer sandwich" or in the high liturgies of other traditions. Not only was this man stepping out in faith and asking for God's healing, but as the minister in this case I was also being challenged. What was I going to do about it? Where was my faith? For those of us in positions of leadership, it's very easy to have everything stitched up so neatly that we rarely actually leave space for ourselves to be challenged. We tend to like everything to be under close control, and to make sure it stays that way.

The condition is almost endemic in Western churches. I shall never forget one occasion when I was leading worship at a Sunday morning service in my own church back in the 1980s, and giving my order of service to the senior minister in advance. He noticed that I had included a point in the service where I was planning to pray specifically with him and for his ministry. With a decisive flourish, he pulled a pen from his pocket and put a stroke through that item, assuring me that "I don't need prayer," and implying that if I did, that was probably because I was inadequate, or a woman—or a clown! We seem to find it incredibly difficult to receive help from one another. But remember Jesus and the woman at the well? Before he was able to share any of his teaching with her, he first received her cup of water.

Many people responded to God that night by Green Lake. I saw people take their shoes off and have crosses painted on their feet, hold out their hands, even ask to have the cross painted on their mouths, and each one in turn was prayed with. Striking and moving though it was, far more went on that night than appeared on the surface. A year or two later, I received an e-mail from an American couple, Dennis and Diane Plourde, working in the Philippines. It so happened that they had stayed in our home the summer before they went to the Philippines, while they were in Scotland on study leave and we were visiting Fuller Seminary. As a thank you for our hospitality, Diane had painted an oil portrait of me in my Valentine clown costume. I was truly delighted with this, and it still hangs in an exalted position. But then, months later, when they had settled into their new surroundings, they met another couple who had also gone to work in the Philippines, and invited them to their home. Diane must have been proud of her painting too, because they had a photograph of it hanging in their living room. The visitor took one look at it and told them exactly who it was, which quite astonished them. Sure enough, he did know who it was, and he had met me. For he was one of the crowd on that night in Wisconsin who had not only been challenged by my invitation to see the world the way God sees it, but had responded by having the cross painted on him—and had gone on to reflect on what it might all mean for his life and ministry. Because of that, he and his family found themselves leaving their home and going to the Philippines.

A favorite metaphor among writers on faith development has often been the idea that nurturing faith is not so much about giving people a finished painting, but providing them with the materials to design their own. A report on children's ministry in British churches once observed that church teachers "know the resources but not the use which will be made of them. What we pass on . . . is not the painting but the paint box."[14] Having, quite literally, handed people the paint box, I can vouch for the truth of that!

Dancing the Truth

I have mentioned some of the history of Mount Zion Church in Jamaica in a previous chapter. But it is more than a historical site. It was a midweek afternoon when I visited it, and there was a meeting in progress, with about twenty or thirty women having animated discussions about what they might do at an outing to the beach that they were planning. These women lived in rural locations spread out all over the forests and hills of that area, and some had walked for an hour or more just to be there, and would walk the same distance back again. They had very few outings so this was a special occasion for them that had been made possible only by a member of the congregation who was also the manager of one of the large beach complexes. You might have thought that the beach would be a natural resource freely accessible to the inhabitants of a Caribbean island, but not in this case. The beaches have mostly been bought up by Western holiday companies and hotel chains, who effectively turn them into fortresses patrolled by armed guards, in order to provide safe havens for the rich white tourists who arrive in liners and stay for a day or two at a time, spending a few hours at the beach.

Up to this point, the women had been engaged in a vigorous debate as to whether or not they would have ice cream during the course of their trip, but once we arrived it was inevitable that we should be drawn into their conversations—and since their minister, Margaret Fowler, was now present, there was also an expectation that she would say something about a passage of scripture that they had also been reading. She had developed a real capacity for affirming these women without taking over, and she neatly sidestepped the expectation that there might be a sermon and introduced me and John instead.

The women were fascinated to know that we were from Scotland, and when they discovered that we had also spent the previous week in the presence of the great and good of their denomination, it was obvious that we were the nearest thing to visitors from heaven. We began to tell them what we had all been doing at the conference. Telling stories came naturally to them, and so they were curious to hear about it—especially when we let slip that the General Secretary of their denomination had been dancing. When they heard that this was something to do with worship and evangelism as well, they could hardly contain their excitement, and they began asking all about it. It was only a matter of time before one of them tentatively asked if they too might be able to explore some of this. We were already standing roughly in a circle, and we soon made a bigger space by moving back some of the pews. Shortly we were all holding hands, singing, dancing—and talking theology, as we explored how circle dancing can be a celebration of God's presence in the midst of people, God in the center of our worship, giving visible form to our belief in incarnation (more prosaically expressed as God's "immanence" for those who like jargon).

After a while we taught them a song that was new to them, which we had first learned from some African Christians ("Hold somebody, tell them that you love them—lift your hands together and praise the Lord"). This is a line dance—which is about God being powerful, God leading us on, God being able to change things ("transcendence"). After we had done this in a kind of conga around the church a few times, the woman who was at the head of the line made a courageous move: she took us out of the church door. The village street was busy with children coming home from school, women carrying water, and men returning from work in the fields. The women were thrilled, because others whom they knew stopped to see what all the commotion was about and to join in the fun for themselves. They caught a glimpse of what could easily happen when celebration of faith becomes mission.

But in the process, they also resolved the matter of what to do on their picnic at the beach. They had previously expressed misgivings about how they might fit in there. Sunbathing had little appeal for them, and in any case these were women whose bodies bore all the signs of years of hard work in the sun, and which would never fit into a trendy bikini. Even if they did, they knew they wouldn't look right. They had been thinking they might feel embarrassed by all the wealthy tourists, but now they knew what they would do. Yes, they would take these dances to the beach, praising God as they did so, and share their faith with whomever else happened to be there. My one regret was that I wasn't staying for long enough to be able to join them.

PART 3

Putting It into Practice

Chapter 10

Getting from Here to There

If you have got this far, you may be wondering how it might be possible to begin to introduce anything remotely like clowning—not to mention mask making, dance, or any of the other things mentioned here—into the life of your own church. Well, there are no easy answers to a question like that, and certainly no single formula or model that can be taken and simply applied across the board. The way things happen varies so enormously from one denomination to another, and even between different parishes and congregations within the same tradition, that I have learned never to be prescriptive when giving advice to others. Not only do things vary from church to church, but it probably also makes a difference whether you are a leader or a member of the congregation. Different people will have different opportunities, so what I want to do here is to share some ideas that I have used myself, together with a few more encouraging stories about churches that have explored this kind of ministry.

While I am firmly committed to pushing forward the frontiers, when it comes to helping churches move on, it is always important to begin where people are at. Activists of all kinds should always remember that and, however strongly they may feel, resist the temptation deliberately to undermine the starting points of other people. There is a definite knack, probably related to individual temperament as much as anything, in being able to live with what the church now does while helping to open up new spaces in which God can work in different ways. I have already indicated in an earlier chapter that the deductive method of traditional theology doesn't specially appeal to me personally, but having said that I do recognize that this is where many people still begin. Before they are going to explore anything as different as Christian clowning—or the arts more generally—they need to be reassured that it is all firmly grounded in what can be recognized as fundamental Christian beliefs and values. A moment's reflection on the previous chapters will demonstrate that this is indeed the case with clown ministry: it emphasizes and grows out of some quite basic doctrines, including a creation-centered spirituality, the incarnation, the cross, resurrection, and the gift of the Holy Spirit, not to mention the church as a community called into existence by what God has done through the person of Jesus Christ.

Rationale for the Creative Arts

It is possible in addition to give some quite specific reasons why the Church ought to be exploring aspects of creativity in relation to its worship and witness today. At least six factors need to be given some consideration.

We live in a visual and tactile age

For much of the 20th century, mission strategists expended enormous energy in working out how the gospel might be contextualized within different cultures all over the world. There is now a very urgent need for Christian faith to be contextualized in Western culture. Since the 1960s, we have moved from a passive literate culture to a highly interactive visual one, but the Church is still largely locked into the culture that has now passed. Indeed, some recent commentators are claiming that we are now in the process of leaving behind the visual culture and moving into what might be called an experience culture, motivated by the search for transformational experiences.

Even when Christians are aware of all this, and the consequent need to develop more relevant models of communication, they still generally stick with words as the most appropriate medium. But as long ago as 1971, the research of Albert Mehrabian was reminding us that only seven per cent of the total impact of any message derives from its words: 38 per cent is from vocal messages (tone of voice), and a massive 55 per cent is non-verbal (body language).[15] To be truly relevant—to those within the Church as well as those who are not yet Christians—we need to contextualize the gospel in contemporary lifestyles.

The Church has been dominated by secular values

For at least the last three hundred years or so, the Church has unwittingly imbibed what are essentially secular ways of doing things. These have mostly been related to the values of the European Enlightenment, especially its habit of elevating what is rational over the intuitional or emotional. René Descartes's definition of what it means to be human ("I think, therefore I am") has, for Reformed and evangelical Christians in particular, come to encapsulate the core of the spiritual life. This has led to a very unbalanced form of Christian faith in which everything has become very bookish. Paradoxically, the use of literature and rational argument to promote the Christian faith was, in its day, at the cutting edge of mission. But we seem to have bought into this not merely as a missiological tool but also as an essential part of our worldview, and Christians easily find themselves promoting some of the most dehumanizing aspects of the Enlightenment philosophy. At a time when even secularists are rediscovering the fundamental importance of emotions and relationships—and as a consequence are themselves becoming more spiritually oriented—there is an urgent need for Christians to find ways of affirming the wholeness of the human person that will be rooted in the values of the gospel rather than (as is often the case in the alternative spiritualities now on offer) in purely humanistic endeavors.

People are suffering

In the post-modern situation, increasing numbers of people are experiencing directly the discontinuities of our culture through personal suffering and the breakdown of their relationships and lifestyles. There is a great need today for emotional healing and wholeness, and that is just as true among those who are Christians as it is for those who are not. People find such needs hard to articulate in words, but experience shows that the creative arts have a unique potential for beginning to address those needs in non-verbal ways. Many of the stories I have shared in previous chapters are really stories of healing, especially those related to painting the cross and empowering people to "see the world the way God sees it." In some cases, I have found myself ministering to people who have spent years in therapy trying to deal with personal baggage of various sorts, only to discover that a very simple tactile thing is able to address their needs far more effectively than any amount of more cognitive understanding.

The arts take the Church back to its heritage

None of this is new: on the contrary, it is a rediscovery of long-forgotten aspects of the Christian tradition. I have already mentioned the fact that Christian clowning, for example, can be traced back to the fourth-century clown Philemon, though in reality it goes much further back than that. The Old Testament prophets were certainly actors, and quite often mimes and clowns. Ezekiel was dumb for much of his ministry, so what did he do? He mimed, of course—using some fairly bizarre techniques in the process (Ezekiel 4:1-8; 5:1-4, among many other passages). But he was not the only one: Jeremiah used all sorts of props, including loincloths (13:1-14), pottery (18:1—19:15), goblets of wine (25:15-36), stones (43:8-13), scrolls (51:62-64) and yokes (27:1—28:17). The history books of the Old Testament contain reports of similar phenomena (1 Kings 11:30-40; 2 Kings 13:15-19, among other passages), while the prophet Isaiah on one famous occasion mimed entirely in the nude (Isaiah

20:1-6). Jesus, of course, was a storyteller, and certainly no stranger to humor.

In centuries of theology dominated by more abstract philosophical categories, important dimensions of the biblical psyche have been obscured. The biblical worldview was much more sensuous, feeling and holistic than the Greek outlook that superseded it. For this reason, the use of our creativity also has the power to unlock hidden dimensions of the Bible itself. Whereas some methods of studying the Bible have tended to ask only historical and literary questions, a more interactive engagement with the text offers unique possibilities for making effective connections with its emotions and practical spirituality. We will return to this shortly.

We need to reclaim some neglected doctrines

Theologically, the current interest in the arts is part of a wider reclamation of belief in the doctrines of creation and incarnation. These have often been marginalized in favor of redemption and atonement, something that no doubt explains why many Christians find the somber seriousness of Lent and Easter easier to handle than the joy of Advent and Christmas. In reality, both perspectives are inextricably bound up with each other, though there can be no doubt that a renewed emphasis on creation and incarnation does raise some fairly radical questions about the nature of Christian faith, particularly our understanding of sin and blessing—questions that would take us well beyond our immediate concerns here, but which have been hinted at and unpacked at different points throughout the previous chapters.

We need to learn from others

Predominantly, Western Christians need to remember that they are no longer a majority of the world's Christians, and that believers in other cultures have often been able to discover new ways to celebrate life and faith in a more holistic fashion, not least in relation to dance and other folk arts. We need to learn from them—and in the process, again reclaim some of our own cultural heritage. Clowning is one example of this, but so are things like

Christmas carols, which derive directly from traditional folk dance in Western culture—over the years we have discarded the movement while keeping the words.

"All That We Are . . . All That God Is"

With these thoughts in mind, where might we start in the average church? First of all, never imagine that you are the wrong person to be able to make a difference. People with an artistic bent can easily allow themselves to be intimidated by those who seem to have had more education, or to be more erudite. Mostly, they have just had a different kind of education. Both you and they are people made in God's image, and that should be the starting point. Of course, you should also read up whatever accessible material you can find—and never forget or downplay the importance of prayer. Identify others you know who might have an interest in similar concerns, and be realistic about where your own community of faith finds itself. Though parish audits were a trendy feature of church life in the 1990s, very few congregations actually have a clear understanding of who they are, and spending some time to reflect on that can actually become a significant process of growth in itself. In working with churches all over the world to help them find new directions, I often find it helpful to get a congregation to describe themselves. Ask a very simple question, such as "Who am I?" In a brainstorming session focused around that, you might typically get a list something like the following:

brother	young	African	European	blind
sister	athletic	good-looking	American	married
mom	single	heterosexual	divorced	single mother
dad	gay	Asian	brainy	creative
cousin	grandma	grandpa	step-child	step-parent
positive	musical	artistic	shy	arrogant
stubborn	quick	slow	caring	awkward

A list like this could be endless. I always tell people that it's all right to include religious expressions, but it is important to list everything about themselves, not just things that might appear to have a religious veneer about them. Some people can't help it, and go into religious jargon right away: you can always make it fun by inviting people to make a farmyard noise like "moo" or "hee-haw" every time someone forgets. It can help to lighten things up: after all, spirituality should be fun! The point is that everyone is encouraged to say exactly what they want. If you are describing yourself, you must be the best person to know—but it takes a trusting group and the creation of a safe space for people to be able to describe themselves in ways that will be more than just predictable.

A couple of practical hints here: it's worth making people stick to only single words for this; and it is better not hurried. You can start in a workshop, but then leave the lists on display some-where for a week or two, so that people can add other things as they engage in further reflection. You can also give people their personal copy of the list, or encourage them to keep their own notebook so that they can add to it at other times and then update the master copy with their new reflections when they meet together again.

You can then move on to ask a slightly different, though related, question: "Who are we?" Who we are as a community or a group will obviously include all the things that we believe our-selves to be as individuals, but addressing the question like this will also lead to a slightly different way of putting things, proba-bly with some items added. When this has been done—and it could take place in special workshops, say on a Saturday, or at a weekend away, or as part of a series doing a different thing each week—it's time to move on and ask a different kind of question: "Who is God?" This can be really illuminating as we discover one another's view of God. Most people will start thinking in big words and traditional theological terminology. But again, it's important to explore all aspects of the ways different people imagine and experience God for themselves. On one occasion when I was doing this, I was intrigued when a woman described herself as "stubborn," and when she came to God she also described God as "stubborn." I thought that was very perceptive: like most characteristics, stubbornness can lead to the kind of awkwardness that can be unhelpful, or it can produce tenacity, which can be a winner. Growth and maturity is about our characteristics being developed in a way that is Godward.

I often find that churches invite me to help them find new ways to worship because they realize the importance of starting with the security of something they already do in order to explore things that might seem more threatening. Since a key purpose of Christian life is, in any case, the worship of God, that is always a good place to begin. I like to suggest to people my own definition of "worship" as being "All that we are, responding to all that God is." Expressing it like that, worship becomes the sum of those things in the first two charts responding to the sum of all those in the third.

It is generally self-evident that we can never address all of these things in a service lasting for an hour or so, and appreciating that limitation can often enable a congregation to see the need for more diversity overall, within a context of a more narrowly defined focus for what we might do on any specific occasion. But the one thing that is absolutely clear is that if we are talking about the whole of our persons responding to the whole of God, then we must include more than just the things that we can think about in abstractions. We need to address all our senses and feelings. Thinking is not to be discouraged, for we are rational beings and as Christians we are called to be transformed "by the renewing of our minds" (Romans 12:2). But by looking at "who we are" in this way, people readily identify for themselves the way in which we have too often focused on analytical thinking to the exclusion of everything else, and that kind of self-discovery can be invaluable as a starting point for exploring how we might redress the balance. Many people will be resistant to hearing it from me, because it can sound like unfair criticism, but giving the chance to explore it for themselves creates a safer space in which, because neither I nor anyone else can predetermine the outcome, the Spirit of God can more easily work to challenge as well as to encourage.

Holistic spirituality

A passage that I have used to stimulate further biblical reflection is Mark 12:28-31, where Jesus reiterates and expands the Jewish statement of faith known as the Shema: "You shall love the Lord your God with all your heart, and with all your soul, and with all your strength" (Deuteronomy 6:5). Interestingly, Jesus added the "mind" to this, though in so doing he did not exclude the other aspects of traditional spirituality—heart, soul, and strength. This is a very holistic way of speaking of the whole of the human personality, including of course the body. Moreover, Jesus links all this to the demand that his disciples should "love your neighbor as yourself"—something also demanded in the Old Testament law, though not in the same place (Leviticus 19:18). Many Christians have a poor self-image, full of guilt, and the last thing they do is love themselves. The first bit of good news, therefore, is that God loves us. We are made in God's image, and the coming of Jesus into the world was God's way of restoring that image through the life, death and resurrection of Christ. Relevant witness, as well as renewed worship, invites us to love ourselves, and then the loving of our neighbor—and the effective celebration of the love of God—will not be nearly such huge problems as they can seem to be.

Since I might easily share my own story in such a workshop, this kind of reflection is not a diversion but is at the very heart of what I want to say, and how I want to see other people empowered. For it was when I was at the very end of myself, incapable of accepting myself—let alone loving what I saw—that I discovered again that God truly loved me, and the broken pieces began to be mended. This sense of vulnerability is probably crucial to the successful integration of the arts into the life of the Church. If we try to promote something merely because we like it, or because it seems trendy, it is easy for things to become a battle of wills between different pressure groups in the Church. But if it emerges out of an honest exploration of who we are, and who God might yet enable us to be, that sets the agenda in a different way altogether.

It is a matter of using the arts with integrity, rather than (as frequently happens) as a gimmick. Whatever the medium might be—drama, mime, painting, sculpting, music, clowning, dance, or anything else you can imagine—it is vital to allow the creative medium to tell its own story and communicate the message. Sometimes I see or hear a good presentation, which will then be followed by a speaker who feels the need to inform the audience or congregation what its "real message" was meant to be. If the art form is not communicating the message in the first place, then why are we using it at all? Moreover, it is an equally pointless exercise to use something artistic as a carrot to attract those whom we might otherwise be unable to pull into church events. Christians seem to imagine that if they brighten things up with a bit of drama, people will come in, and once inside they can hear the "real" message—usually in the form of a sermon. This kind of thinking denigrates the sermon as well as the art. People are not so easily fooled, and though they may be hoodwinked once, they are unlikely to be taken in a second time. The creative and expressive arts are part of the way we as God's people communicate and express our relationship with God and as such they should not be squeezed into some other mould.

Chapter 11

Start with Something Simple

All churches have services, and since it's good to start where people are, this for most of us will be the place. Think, for instance, of some of the things that are typically included in all services—prayers and readings. What are some of the things you could creatively do with these? The actual answer will depend on what you are already doing.

Prayer

Prayer is a comfortable place for most congregations to begin, and creative ideas do not need to be wacky ideas. For example, in churches that have no regular liturgy, something as simple as having responsive prayers could be a whole new concept—or something as simple as inviting the congregation to shout out the things they would like to give thanks for while someone writes them up on an overhead projector, to make a list from which the leader can then group the various things together. Doing this demands a bit of creativity, so that such prayers are not read out like a shopping list, nor for that matter in a pompous way with lots of flowery language.

A little experimentation will soon show who is good at this kind of thing, and who should be asked to do something else. As you experiment, you may well discover someone who doesn't usually take a leading role, but who has perhaps spent years praying and in the process has developed a rich and spontaneous vocabulary in expressing themselves to God, while still being readily accessible to others. Incorporating a response can further enhance the community's ownership of the prayer, but the most significant thing is that this method ensures that it is not just the favorite subjects of the leaders that are reflected upon, but the concerns of a far wider group. On another occasion, you could list requests for God—territory in which it is even more important to resist the temptation to address God as a shop assistant.

A format that I have never known to fail is to get a family to pray. I remember once talking about this to my local ministers' fraternal organization (and they were all "fraternal"—I was the only woman). One other minister immediately commented that it would be important to exercise care in choosing the right kind of family. For him, a single-parent family would have been the "wrong" sort, as also no doubt would have been a blended family created by partners with children from previous relationships, or indeed a couple without children. With half of all marriages in Britain now ending in divorce, and increasing numbers of people finding themselves childless, both by choice and otherwise, this probably highlights one of the reasons why many churches find it so difficult to relate to the wider community. But in addition, remember that a family can consist of more than just adults, and if all members of a household pray, they are likely to reflect a broader spectrum of life issues than if only the parents or other adults do.

I remember suggesting this to one of my friends, who tried it by asking a family where Dad was a surgeon, Mom a teacher, and the four teenagers were all bright kids. The church enjoyed the way they led the prayers together, but even more interesting was the fact that when the minister called to thank them, the family said that it was the best piece of pastoral care they had ever received because asking them to lead the prayers had required that they all sit down together and talk to one another. Different families will bring different perspectives, which is good. And of course, when I write "family" I am also aware that the family of God consists not only of parents and children, but also single people, older people and so on. Make sure they are all represented.

Once people are familiar with more relaxed forms of prayer, invite them to talk in small groups and to pray for each other. This can move churches forward with a big leap, and I have only ever found one congregation that reacted negatively to this. Interestingly, it was the church I have already mentioned in chapter 9, where the senior minister told me not to pray for him. I was leading a section of all-age worship in the service over a period of five weeks, and I decided to explore different forms of prayer each week. I can't now recall all the things I did, but they were probably mostly along the lines of what I have described here. I certainly won't forget the week when I invited the congregation to share in small groups. When the doorbell at home rang the next morning while I was still in the shower, I grabbed my toweling robe and ran downstairs at top speed, expecting it to be the postal delivery. But it was this same senior minister, and I thought there must at least be a major world disaster for him to be standing on my doorstep so early on a Monday morning. He brought bad news—that "some people" had been shocked by being asked to pray with others like that. At the time, I recognized his sense of embarrassment (and also knew that "some people" can be a regular euphemism for whoever is speaking), and offered not to continue with the series, something to which he agreed with enthusiasm. But on reflection, I remembered that this was the same man who, not long before, had forbidden me to pray for him in the service. Maybe this was a case of the medium being the message. Integrity is certainly important in ministry, and in a negative sort of way this individual had integrity: the message had got through to his congregation that, because he didn't need prayer, neither did they.

Prayer is also an easy point at which to introduce clowning into worship. One of my most vivid memories of this was at the Salvation Army in Leicester, which I must have visited at an early stage in my ministry. I was the only clown (as Valentine—my only character at that time), and I needed a helper. As I stood hanging about at the back of the building, waiting for the appropriate moment in the service, a little boy crept in late, and I asked him if he would help. He was the nearest thing I could imagine to Oliver from Charles Dickens's famous novel, and was one of the most natural performers I have ever worked with. In the sketch I was planning, I had a large newspaper tucked under my arm, and the idea was that we would chat to one another as we walked slowly to the front of the church, making comments on the people and things around us, before sitting down on a bench to read the paper.[16] As I open the newspaper, I make random observations about the day's news, and my colleague hopefully contributes relevant responses—which this small boy did wonderfully. As it opens, it becomes obvious that this is no ordinary newspaper but a specially constructed clown's paper that gets bigger and bigger all the time. As you can imagine, this provides plenty of scope for slapstick humor at the same time as the serious matters of the day are being highlighted. Eventually the clown gets in an awful muddle, and the paper is torn and crumpled before being screwed up into a large ball and thrown to whoever is leading the service with a comment like, "Have you read the news yet? I can't do anything with it—see if you can." When the leader stands in a sideways profile to hold the paper, it looks just like a huge, round and very messy world—a strong visual image—which can then be used as a focus for prayer.

People who were at the service still have difficulty believing that this little boy was not some child I had adorned with makeup to look like a tramp character. But he was definitely the real thing. Later on, he sat next to me on the floor at the back and we played tiddlywinks with the ringpulls from drink cans that he had in his pocket. When the time for the offering came, he had nothing to put in and I only had three juggling balls. I whispered to him, "Do you think they would have these?" He wasn't sure, but I put them in anyway and when the offering was taken to the front on large plates, everyone saw the juggling balls on top of the pile. Fortunately for me, the woman leading the service was well tuned in to God's creative Spirit and she prayed that God would take all our money and our talents to use in the work of the kingdom.

Another interesting thing happened that day too. The church building was in an area with a large Asian population, and as soon as I emerged from the church at the end of the service, the Muslim shopkeepers waved and crossed the road, keen to engage me in conversation and have me visit their premises. I think the regular Salvation Army people were amazed, because they had been trying to make contact with these very same people and had found it incredibly difficult to bridge the barriers not of race, but of suspicion. For the local people, a uniform spoke of authority and invoked fears of official investigations and possible persecution. But a clown . . . well, let's just say it reminded me again of the importance of the medium being the message.

Another thing I often do is to use bubbles in prayer, something I first learned from Roly Bain, a full-time Anglican clown priest. If you put some in a child's Christmas stocking, you will have no problem having a prayer time even on Christmas day! In church I have used them both with clown costume and without. This works more easily with two people, one to blow the bubbles while the other speaks. As the bubbles are blown, you can talk about them being fragile and disappearing into space—a bit like our prayers. Some are small, like some of our problems—others can represent friends, or sick people, and a big bubble blown specially can be a "thank you" for Jesus. This can be a very quiet and moving experience because of course people keep their eyes open to watch the bubbles instead of having their heads bowed. The movement of the bubbles will depend on the air currents and humidity. Sometimes they will sail away into the roof and lift our eyes heavenward, at other times they will fall and burst on the ground. In either case, we need to be aware of what's going on and connect with it. I sometimes use a simple response such as, "As the bubbles fall to the ground and burst, we know God is hearing our prayers." I remember once using bubbles for prayer in a Methodist church on the island of

Guernsey, which had a really huge pulpit from where I blew them. At the end, an older woman came to me and said "I have never been so moved by the prayers in church." It was the week that important school exams were starting, and among other things I used them to pray for all the kids who would be sitting for the exams.

Teenagers can find church quite hard to fit into and adults don't always know how to be able to affirm them without seeming to be patronizing. Exam time at school is very pressured: children see their whole future depending on their performance, and can easily be overwhelmed by it all. An older woman in a church I belonged to for a long time has single-handedly worked at this for several years. She makes time to find out when every child has important exams and then she lists them on a sheet showing when all the exams take place, and hands the list to the congregation as an invitation to pray for the teenagers all by name at relevant moments. When the young people go off to university, she stays in contact by sending little cards to encourage them. In a day when most teenagers find it difficult to connect with a different generation, she has found a most effective way of doing this without overwhelming them. One time when John and I were away speaking at a conference, she invited our son Mark over for dinner and they played chess together, which may seem a very little thing—quaint, even—but it certainly impressed him as a teenager, even though he's probably never played chess since. This particular woman formerly held a senior position in nursing, though she has been retired now for a good number of years and probably imagines she has little in common with today's teenagers. But she has a caring heart. In fact, as I reflect on this story I recall that she was working in the hospital the morning after Mark was born, and she came and prayed with me to share my joy. She was well placed to do so as she had also sat with us in a hospital ward sharing our pain following the death of our previous child.

Creative Bible Reading

Creative Bible reading is another good entry point for introducing new ways of doing things in the life of the church. At a very simple level, there is *The Dramatized Bible,* which provides interactive scripts for responsive readings covering the entire Bible, from Genesis to Revelation—using the actual words of commonly used Bible versions.[17]

There is, however, a more ambitious way of exploring the Bible that I have often used, and found to be widely acceptable even in regular Sunday services. This is a technique that I first learned from the Jesuit scholar, Michael Moynahan, when I was studying at the Graduate Theological Union in Berkeley, California, and since then I have refined and adapted it in my own way. The idea is for a small group of four to six people to take a Bible story and create somewhere between four and six still-life pictures from the story. They then work out how to put themselves in the frame and create each of these still-life pictures as a tableau, each one held for a minute or two in turn by the participants turning themselves into statues. The rest of the group forms the audience, who are instructed to put their "curtains down" (close their eyes) while the performers rearrange themselves in between each change of scene.

It takes maybe fifteen to twenty minutes for a group to read a story and then reimagine it in this way, and as they do so I frequently hear them arguing about what the Bible actually says, in a way that drives them back to read the text for themselves in order to get the accurate information. This is one of the best motivators for serious Bible study I have yet discovered. It can be done with almost any number of people, because even a large crowd can divide into small groups and then come together and present their stills to one another. It becomes great fun as people test one another's Bible knowledge by seeing how easy or difficult it is to guess what others have been working on. It can also highlight the unconscious assumptions that we make, showing us that we are not communicating what we thought we were, which can provide the opportunity to make adjustments.

Sometimes, I like to throw in a story that is not from the Bible, as a way of injecting more fun but also emphasizing some serious theological reflection on the nature of evangelism. Sleeping Beauty is a favorite one for this purpose, and even though I wouldn't deliberately imply that this is a Bible story, when watching a presentation of it people will often identify it with the raising of Lazarus, or even the resurrection of Jesus. As they ponder such connections, important lessons are being learned about the spiritual search of our culture and the ways in which we need to be ready to place the everyday stories of ordinary people alongside the Bible stories, in order that they might all be transformed in the light of the even bigger story of what God is doing in the lives of us all. More information about this, and some instructions and guidelines for using this approach, are included in appendix 1 at the end of the book.

Once you've tried the stills, you can take it a stage further and make a moving tableau. My favorite—and certainly a good one to start with—is the story of Jesus in the boat when the storm starts up (Mark 4:35-41). I like it best because it's the first one I was ever part of, and what I learned from it has stuck with me ever since. It was my very first week in California, and Michael Moynahan had us do this exercise in his class. As I wondered who I might be in the story, I decided just to be a little wave somewhere on the edge, and contentedly watched as others took dominant roles. But in the subsequent reflection I learned a lot—about myself as well as about the Bible story. I realized that my choice to be a little wave on the edge actually corresponded with exactly how I was feeling right then. I was in a foreign land, struggling with more culture shock than I wanted to admit, and for that reason not really a part of the group and totally lacking in confidence.

As I have used this same technique for Bible study elsewhere, I have seen others have similar learning experiences about their own circumstances. I remember exploring the story of Luke 5:1-11 with a church in Scotland. This is the account of the disciples working all night but catching no fish, and then Jesus sending them out again, whereupon they made a great catch. The people in this particular church threw themselves into it with great energy, with a boat full of people working their hardest while others were on the periphery as waves, fish, and so on. When we came to unpack the experience, those who had been in the boat put their lack of success down to the fact that there was nothing to be caught, but others (who had been the fish) couldn't agree. "There were plenty of fish," they told them, "but they were all on the other side of the boat. You were just fishing in the wrong place." In the course of further reflection on this, they started to discover for themselves all sorts of things about their concern for evangelism, and began to wonder if some of their lack of success was not so much because the things they were doing were wrong, but because their activities were just irrelevant to their particular community at that time.

I later incorporated this methodology into some all-age liturgies I was producing for Scripture Union's worship publications, and one day I found myself accosted in the middle of my grocery shopping by a minister who came running down the aisle in the supermarket shouting, "We did it in our church—and we all loved it!" much to the surprise of the other shoppers. The interesting thing about taking this approach in an intergenerational setting is that older people, even those with little mobility, can be included. It's one of the few contexts where a person in a wheelchair can take the leading role just as easily as anyone else. Allow people to choose to fit into the scene wherever they wish, and then for a few minutes act out the scene together while you get a rhythm going. But you'll almost always need more time than you think for people to talk through the experience later. A lot of informed learning can take place at both an individual and a community level.

Another step on from this is to make a movie—not with a real camera, just acting. Have someone operating the imaginary camera, calling the takes, and then invite people to enter into the scene when they feel ready. Define a specific line so that they know they have entered the movie scene when they choose to cross it. It's good to start off with something that's not particularly religious, like a party or a market, or some other activity that everyone will easily enter into. The reason for doing this is that in a "normal" scene people will typically act at a high level of energy, and it's important to keep that same level of energy when the transition is made into a Bible story. For some reason, people instinctively move into a different—less imaginative—mode for that. One church I did this with created a wonderful market scene to begin with, and then I suggested they change gear and move into the Sermon on the Mount. The minister was the first one into the scene. It was something he felt comfortable with, and as he walked up the imaginary hill, the others automatically followed him and sat down to listen. When someone called out, "some things never change," he got the message! In fact, he knew the message to start with, but he wouldn't have thought he was the kind always to assume control until our "movie making" created the space for him to see himself the way others do.

I remember working the film sequence in a class at Fuller Seminary when one of the students told me that he was a film director. In Los Angeles, that could mean anything, because it sometimes seems that everybody claims some sort of connection with the movie industry. But when he told me some of the films he had directed, even I was impressed because they were well-known blockbusters. I wondered why I was trying to teach this technique to the class when he was there, so I invited him to show us how he would do it. He pushed us a lot further than I would have done, because he decided to do the crucifixion. I would certainly have gone for something safer. Anyway, he set up the three key figures on crosses, the women at the foot of the cross, and the crowd. Normally we don't take too much notice of the crowd. "Let's hear what you would shout," he said. The noise rose, and some found it very challenging. Soon one person went over the edge and found herself laughing with embarrassment, but even that led to an interesting piece of learning. "Don't worry," our director said, "in the movies, when we can't get the actors to cry, we just get them to laugh and do a voiceover." That rang true for us all. Crying often borders on laughter, and vice versa. We all learned something about our emotions that day, as well as having a lesson in how to defuse a potentially embarrassing situation very smoothly.

Creative exploration of Bible stories can also be a good way to relate to the wider community beyond the Church. A year or two ago, I visited a small town in the state of New Hampshire. Like many American settlements it displays its population on the sign that welcomes the visitor—and this one numbered its people in hundreds, not thousands. In appearance, it was just like a movie set—think of *The Waltons* or *Little House on the Prairie*, and you've got the picture. There were white clapboard homes, with a central crossroads at which the railroad crossed the main street. On one corner was the town hall, on another corner the part-time fire station, on another the post office, and on the other a church. The church was also constructed of white-painted clapboard, including its steeple, and the minister was also the local fire chief, as well as the key holder for all the other important buildings in the community.

It was a sleepy, idyllic place to live—but not, you might imagine, a place where innovation was likely to flourish in the church. Well, you'd be wrong. It's not that their Sunday services are especially trendy—they're actually quite traditional. Nor is the church full of young people: it's the kind of area to which people retire, though there are some younger ones. But for several years now they've drawn significant crowds throughout Advent. They decided to do something very simple—to tell the Christmas story to their community. Outside the church they set up a backdrop, they use a tape of the Christmas story which can be amplified, and as the story progresses all the characters gradually emerge, dressed in appropriate clothing, and step into the tableau until the complete narrative has been both told and seen. Remember, New Hampshire is very cold in December. Most years, this outdoor tableau is presented in several feet of snow. But it happens each evening during Advent, taking about twenty minutes each time—and it causes traffic jams as people from miles around come in their cars to be part of the celebration.

To do this in most places in Britain would require a slightly different set-up. In towns and cities, shopping centers may be a more appropriate venue—or, in city center churches, just outside the church itself. In the country or the suburbs, something similar to the New Hampshire project might easily work. In fact, not long after I visited that church, I unexpectedly had the opportunity to do something similar in my own church back home—something I have included at the end of the book as appendix 3.

Anyone for Dance?

Once you have explored the Bible in some of these dramatized forms, it is only a short step to including dance. Some people feel threatened by that word, so it can be better to talk about "movement" instead. A passage like the Magnificat is a fine example of one that lends itself easily to this kind of interpretation (Luke 1:46-55). It is not necessary to find someone trained in ballet in order to include dance in worship. Professional dancers can certainly bring their own contribution, but there is a danger that if they are the only ones who dance in worship, it is seen as performance rather than something for the ordinary person to join in. A gentle response to spoken words or song, that comes from the heart and is offered to God with integrity, cannot fail to draw others nearer to God.

It can be a challenge identifying different types of movement, and it is important to include strong actions as well as softer expressions. The one mistake that interpreters of song often make is to include too many repetitive arm movements. You can avoid some of this if a group includes women and men together, and I always try to encourage a new group to set itself up in this way. If only women dance, it very quickly becomes perceived as something that only women do. By contrast, the traditional Jewish dance that has grown most obviously from biblical roots has strong rhythmical movement, and is intended to be community dance, not individual performance.

If a particular congregation is not used to moving, the biggest task can be to create a safe space for people to work out how to do it. Sometimes it is easier to accomplish this at an informal gathering, such as a supper or other social event, where people are likely to be more relaxed and probably more open to trying something different. People can be unbelievably insecure, and generally appreciate being given some specific movements that can inspire confidence in what they are doing and help them to begin to enjoy it. When they have done it once, they will invariably want to participate again. The freeing up of our bodies often leads to the freeing up of other areas of worship that we find hard to know how to address.

Communion is a time when dance by one or two people can be especially meaningful. I remember dancing to the song "Take our bread, we ask you" as a preparation for sharing the Eucharist. The particular Sunday in question happened to be World AIDS Day, and I had my pockets filled with red ribbons, which I threw up in the air as a response to the final words, "Take our lives, oh Father: we are yours, we are yours." Though I hadn't realized in advance that it would happen like this, the ribbons showered down over the bread and wine of communion, and by the time the service was finished, none were left at the table: there had obviously been a dynamic of response and commitment created by the visual impact that I certainly could not have anticipated, as the worshipers subsequently took the ribbons with as much enthusiasm as they received the sacrament. To some of them, that probably was the sacrament on that occasion. Certainly, many people in the congregation (which was not one accustomed to seeing this kind of thing happen) found it a most poignant reminder of the identification of Jesus with our pain and suffering, and were profoundly challenged and deeply moved.

In similar vein, I remember once being part of a moving dance that included the symbols of foot-washing. It was at an ordination, and one of my friends played the part of Mary

Magdalene, who, as she experienced Jesus's forgiveness, cast aside her dark shroud, which symbolized the mess in her life. Once forgiven and renewed, Mary moved out with a bowl and water among the congregation and washed the hands of the people she met. On that occasion, I was in the aisle, on the receiving end, and I was one who received the blessing. But so did all the others, for the water in the bowl was scented with lavender, thereby creating a fragrance that spread over the whole church so that everyone in effect became a part of the dance, whether or not they had their hands or feet washed.

Dance does not have to be polished performance in order to address spiritual needs. I remember leading a weekend of workshops for one of the presbyteries of the Church of Scotland, which was to culminate in a service of rededication for the Christian community on the Sunday evening. During the sessions—which were a mixture of thinking and doing—there was one person who, if there was an awkward question to be asked, could be guaranteed to find it. By the end of the very first evening (a Friday) I had mentally labeled him as one of God's troublemakers, and things did not improve the next day. When we all came together on the Sunday afternoon, for our final preparation of the rededication service, we were under a good deal of time pressure, and out of all the participants in the workshop I was left with only a handful of people whom I hadn't managed to include in the service up to that point. Almost as an afterthought, I told them I had brought some flags, and invited the group to see what they could do with them. I don't know if I even consciously expected them to come up with anything at all: I just wanted to find something for everyone.

Anyway, the "awkward" man ended up in that group, and to my great surprise this was just what he was looking for. He was not far off his eightieth birthday, and it turned out that in younger life he had held a senior position in a Scottish Army regiment. As he said, flags were just his thing: he'd spent much of his life marching behind them on parade grounds. I wondered whatever he might do next—but there wasn't enough time for me to check it out in advance, so you can imagine how relieved (and amazed) I was that as we all processed into the church to the song "I will enter God's gates with thanksgiving in my heart," he took up pole position at the head of us all, with not one but two flags (one in each hand), waving them in perfect timing and setting exactly the right tone for what was to follow. In fact, throughout the service he was up at the front waving the flags at every opportunity he could find. By the end, all his questions and hesitations had disappeared, not because they were answered in any kind of abstract analytical way, but because he had discovered something that connected with who he was in the rest of his life experience.

Chapter 12

Bring On the Clowns

Perhaps you can see the potential in what I have described in the last two chapters, but full-blown clown ministry seems to be going just too far. This, of course, is the area in which I have most experience, though I included the other suggestions first in order to highlight other possibilities, and to affirm the fact that we all have to begin from the circumstances in which we find ourselves. Inevitably, one thing leads to another, and as people grow more confident in their exploration of new ways to worship—and of being church—you will find that, under God's guidance, even those who look like stick-in-the-muds can become adventurous and forward-looking. Your church may not be ready for clowning today, but who knows what tomorrow might be like?

Thinking It Through
To begin to explore clown ministry, the best way forward is to gather a group who are specifically interested and spend significant time working together, for at least a full day if not a whole weekend. Invite someone who is already working as a Christian clown, preferably someone with a widely varied experience and enough confidence in their own skills not to just persuade you to do all the things they themselves like best. Plan the day well, and take the risk of experimenting without needing to have a

predictable outcome. You should, however, have some sense of a goal that can be achieved within a short space of time. For example, whenever I lead a workshop myself, I generally try to build in the expectation that at least something will be produced that can be incorporated into a Sunday service—or taken into the street.

Clown ministry is an essentially practical thing. This is not to say that there is no reflective or theoretical base to it: I hope that anyone who has read this far will be left in no doubt that quite the reverse is true, and Christian clowning has a very extensive theological and spiritual undergirding. But in the end, it is something to be done rather than just talked about, and getting involved in specific occasions is the only way to actually become a clown, as distinct from being someone who knows a lot about it. In that respect, it's no different from any other form of Christian service or spirituality, of course. Apart from that, participants in a workshop need to be given opportunities for encouragement. Most people—even those trying it for the first time—are capable of much more than they think they are, and are usually astonished at what they have achieved in such a short space of time. This in itself provides more motivation to go on and build on what they have learned.

If you can't find another person with experience in this kind of ministry, but you're keen to explore it for yourself, think about setting up a workshop by yourself. Print colorful invitations and get people to enroll in advance. Decide on the fee to cover the costs and whether or not food will be included. There will always be some costs, so be realistic about this. If you invite someone in to lead the workshop, expect to pay for that—but also don't forget that there will always be costs for materials (makeup, props, and so on). In any case, people tend to value something that they have paid for, and when advance registrations are required they are likely to be committed to actually being there on the day.

Though I have frequently emphasized the need to be open-ended in clown ministry, don't allow that to be an excuse for sloppiness. Any kind of learning experience needs to be appropriately structured. I always set very specific (even detailed) aims and objectives at the beginning, so that people know what they might expect to be able to do by the end. Not only does this give participants a sense of security, but it's also important for keeping the whole enterprise on track: if you don't spell out what you're aiming for, then you will never know whether or not you have achieved your ambitions. Name tags that are worn by everyone are important. I go to far too many events where people have no idea who the others are, and never introduce themselves. You'll never make much progress with a group who stay at arm's length from one another. A good way to enable people to loosen up physically as well as emotionally is to play a few games to start with—not team or competitive games, but fun things that people can enjoy while getting to know the others. Make sure your venue has lots of empty space: this is one of the most important requirements for a successful clown workshop. Do some things that exercise the mind as well as the body.

Most people would expect to put makeup on as the very first thing at a clown workshop. But save it until later. It can provide a change of pace after a lot of play, and though it's great fun it can also be embarrassing for people who've never tried it before. They might well make a terrible mess just because they are inexperienced at working with materials like makeup, though the good news is that you can always take it off and start again. In relation to a clowning workshop, it's important to conclude the event (or each day if it's a weekend) by setting what you have done in the context of thanksgiving and worship.

Don't forget to take photos of the day: you will be surprised in a very short time to look back and see how far you have progressed. You will also be encouraged, as I am whenever I look at some of my earliest clown photos. Affirm people's achievement by awarding them a certificate. They're easy enough to design on a computer, so make some and use them. You'll only be grade 1 at this stage, of course, but that in itself can hold out the promise of more advanced reflection and skills to come.

Be encouraged to search out an experienced clown to help you, for in this kind of work there's nothing quite like the investment of another person who's gone before. They can save you a lot of pitfalls, and you will find them usually happy to help and encourage you. If starting a group looks unlikely, then search out an existing group or individual Christian clown in your area and ask if you can apprentice yourself to them. Learn by helping and doing. Clowns who have worked alongside me in the past have usually started off very unsure, but with gentle encouragement have found themselves almost unwittingly taking on quite challenging tasks till they find they become totally captivated by it.

Don't forget that anyone can try makeup by themselves. So get some and see what kind of clown face you can create. There are numerous books around to give you ideas, but here again there is no substitute for experimenting. It can be worth drawing some face shapes on blank paper and then, with colored pens, filling in differently shaped eyebrows and mouths until you get something that looks as if it might suit you. Try different formats, make changes, ask someone else what they think. The most frequent mistake made by beginners is to apply too much makeup too thickly, and to use too many different colors. Remember that people seeing you from a distance need to be able to distinguish clearly defined lines, and if you overcrowd your face and make it too fussy you will obliterate it rather than making it more visible. Think of mime artists you may have seen, who conventionally wear a completely white face with only minimalist markings in black and red. Their features can be seen from a considerable distance.

The stories told up to this point will, I hope, have stimulated creative ideas and possibilities for you, the reader. All the stories are true, though sometimes I have obscured specific details in order to protect an individual's privacy. Don't be afraid to learn from the experience of other people. I've included lots of stories here for that very reason. But equally, remember that what works for somebody else won't necessarily be the right thing for you. Indeed, I would say from my own experience that you can't assume that what works in one place will automatically transfer to another one. Do your research carefully, and get to know as much as you can about your workshop participants or those who will watch or hear you. Adapt your approach and contextualize the experience so it will have integrity in the circumstances where you are working. And once you start to perform for and with other people, remember two golden rules.

- Give people enough psychological space. Wait to be invited into their space, rather than assuming you have the right to intrude.
- Never forget the importance of affirming people rather than putting them down. That way you can be sure you will be following Jesus.

Planning a Clown Ministry Workshop

I have already given a few general ideas, but to help you get started, here is a suggested schedule for a first time clown workshop. Of course, it is not set in stone, so feel free to adapt it as necessary. But many people tell me they have difficulty with knowing exactly where to start in organizing something like this, so I am including this here as a possible starting point. I am assuming you will have a workshop over a weekend, beginning Friday evening and ending on Sunday.

Before the Event

Don't neglect advance planning: it can be the most important thing of all for ensuring success. Circulate information well ahead of time, and publicize the event well. Set a date and price for enrollment and provide people with a list of things they might like to bring—bright T-shirt, baggy pants, anything they might think suitable for dressing in (but discourage them from spending money on special things in advance). It might be helpful if people bring their own mirror and washing materials.

Arrange the space in a welcoming manner and decorate with balloons and clown paraphernalia. You could use posters of clowns, or a collage of different faces and costumes. Make sure you arrive in good time yourself, and have helpers organized to welcome people and put them at their ease, ensuring that everyone receives a copy of the program layout for the weekend so that they know exactly what to expect.

Friday Evening

7:30 PM: Welcome everyone into a circle and make a game of learning one another's names. Using one bean bag or something similar, make eye contact with someone at another point in the circle, and throw the bean bag to them at the same time as shouting your own name. They in turn will do the same thing, shouting their own name, and so on. Make sure everyone has said their name two or three times, and if anyone is being overlooked make a point of including them without making it too obvious.

Then change tactics. Instead of shouting your own name, shout the name of the person to whom you are throwing the bean bag. Of course you won't get them all right, and this is the first step in encouraging one another. When it's going well, quietly introduce a second bean bag to liven things up a bit. When this is established, include a third and possibly a fourth. Eventually this will turn into mayhem and a lot of laughter, which is exactly what you want. You can now say with some confidence, "We all know one another's names." If the group is large (say, more than 15) it could be worthwhile reinforcing the names by inviting people to arrange themselves in alphabetical order. It's a good time to make a joke that if people have always wanted to change names now is the time to do it.

7:45 PM: You can now get the brains working with another game. Choose to be a vegetable or a fruit and go round the circle (you could sit informally on the floor) saying, "I'm a . . . because . . ."—for example, "I'm a sprout because I keep popping up everywhere," or "I'm a kiwi, rough and hairy on the outside but soft and squashy inside."

People will come up with surprises even at this early stage, which will encourage everyone to realize that this is going to be fun. It can, however, be harder than it sounds, so if anyone is struggling, encourage them. Some will probably feel quite hesitant, but the shy ones who hang back often come up with the most interesting characterizations. Give people plenty of time and let them think before you come back to them if necessary. But if they are really struggling, think of something affirming and true to say for them, for example, "I think you might be like a strawberry—that's my favorite fruit."

8:00 PM: Now how about playing clown tag, which is just like normal tag where someone is "it," but first you need to explain that this can be done at three settings—slow, normal, and fast forward. Have somebody to shout out commands: "Slow . . . Normal . . . Fast forward . . . Slow . . ." and so on. This will of course be great fun, but already you will have something to unpack. When the game is exhausted and before too many collisions start to occur, sit down and ask how people enjoyed it. Did they notice anything significant? Tease it out, don't blurt out the answers but don't leave people stuck either. When you play clown tag, it is interesting to notice that when we move slowly we are usually quieter than when we run and the noise level increases. This can be commented on and observed in relation to clowning. It's a common misapprehension that good clowning will be even better if it's boisterous. But watch any of the great artists—the way they incline the head, the raising of the eyebrows and so on—and you'll realize there's a lot more subtlety involved than many people realize.

8:30 PM: Try to show a video like *Parable,* which I've already mentioned in an earlier chapter. That would certainly be my first choice, but if it is not available use a filmstrip on clowning or a video of some of the great artists miming or clowning and just have fun. Remember, this is Friday night and people may well be tired from a tough week at work—so it's best not to be too prolonged or heavy.

9:00 PM: Coffee/light supper and chat. If you haven't included prayer, then you might like to do so at this point. Make a definite finish at 9:30 PM so that those who want to can go home without feeling they have missed out. Give specific instructions for Saturday—but keep it short. Close with a shared benediction. Others can stay and socialize for a while if they wish, but remember, you want to encourage everyone to be back for a prompt start in the morning.

If you have opted to offer accommodation to those coming from a distance, make sure they are connected with their hosts and not left hanging around wondering if they should have come. For the same reason, in organizing the games, do it in such a way that cliques can't easily be formed, and look out for each person's low moments.

Saturday

9:30 AM: Start the day with prayer, inviting the Holy Spirit to lead you through this uncharted territory. Maybe make the prayer one that goes round the circle with each person adding just a phrase—though not going round the world in the process!

9:35 AM: A game can be a good idea, particularly if it's winter when church halls can be cold (but don't make games a substitute for proper heating). Parachute games are good here, not least because they enable you to include everyone. I got my first parachute from the RAF, and it is an excellent resource for really large crowds, but you need a minimum of 40-50 people to work with it—and a very large space. You can get lightweight nylon parachutes in a variety of sizes from suppliers of play equipment, and they usually come with suggestions for appropriate games. Everyone stands round the parachute, holding their own section of it, and then the fun begins. After you've got used to the feel of how you might move it (for example, by making it mushroom upwards, changing places by running underneath it), try putting an earth-patterned ball into orbit on the parachute, and send it spinning round the periphery. It will take something like a Mexican wave to get it right—in other words, good teamwork, which is exactly what embryo clowns need the most. As it gets under way, you could join in singing "He's got the whole world in his hands" and add a verse or two that allows you to include everyone there by name.

If you don't have a parachute, how about doing a bathroom routine? Use the tune of "Here we go round the mulberry bush on a cold and frosty morning" (or "on a warm and sunny morning" if that is more appropriate), with each person in turn choosing a phrase and action to match it—for instance, "This is the way we brush our teeth . . ." and so on.

9:45 AM: Here's another game that can be played in pairs facing one another. One person takes the initiative, while the other is to be a reflection in the mirror. Go through your imaginary bathroom routine. It can be as funny as you like, but the secret is to move together so well that people looking on would have difficulty telling who was the real person and who was the mirror. After each couple has done it both ways round, change partners completely and see what happens. If you spot two who are really good at it, affirm them by letting the class watch them for a few minutes. But don't make the mistake of insisting that every couple do this: it would be boring, quite apart from possibly being embarrassing for some.

9:55 AM: Another game is to pretend that everyone is at the bottom of a deep ocean. Now try to move forwards, struggling under the pressure of water and imaginary sea currents. Encourage the group to respond as though it was really tough—if people are walking about normally, then they are not on the ocean floor. Invite participants to make the noises they feel would be appropriate to their struggle or their environment as they move.

10:00 AM: By now, it's probably time for something a bit less strenuous and physically demanding. Find a spot on the floor where people can lie down on their back without touching another person, and preferably with a bit of space around them. Ask the participants to close their eyes, and then create an imaginary scene. This is called creative visualization, and is a technique of painting a picture with words, so the leader needs to practice this in advance. If it helps, write out a description for yourself in advance.

Invite everyone to join you on a walk—take them where you like—through fields or shops, wherever, but describe it graphically. Include the participants' senses by mentioning the smells and noises, and don't forget their sense of touch and taste. Bring your group to an encounter with a clown, whether it be in the circus, in a field or a shopping center—judge which will give them the best visual image depending on who they are. Make sure you encourage your listeners to have a good look at the clown and notice the detail on the costume and face and so on. Let them engage with the clown, before inviting them to go round the back of the clown, unzip their new companion and step into the clown suit themselves. They can then go on a journey together, briefly, and return to the spot they started from, where they will have to get out of costume and lay aside the suit, before shaking hands with their new pal and saying goodbye, promising to remember their clown's name.

It can be a good idea to have some music in the background, although not necessarily all the time. Perhaps, when you introduce the idea of clowns, you could play some clown-like music (there are plenty of specialist recordings of calliope music available). This will allow you to create spaces in your description more easily. Remember, the music will work better if you gradually turn up the volume and slowly fade it out. When the music is fading, let people know that you will give them a few minutes to gather their thoughts and step out of the imaginary world back into the real one. When they are ready, they can open their eyes and sit up.

Before the impact of this exercise is lost, give people colored pens and paper to let them catch something of the clown they were for that brief time. Some will scribble furiously, others will need encouragement—they might say "I didn't see anything," or "I can't draw." It's not the quality of the drawing that counts—it's capturing the ideas that is the important thing. Everyone will have seen something, but they may need a few helpful questions to enable them to tease out what they did see. They may feel awkward that they don't have a complete picture but just one dominant thing. This happened at a workshop I held, and a young man was so excited that he could tell me exactly what sort of shoes he had—with curled toes and bells on, and they were red, either leather or velvet—but that was all. Two years later I met him in Glasgow and he greeted me with, "Hi, I'm the one from the workshop who saw the red shoes. Do you remember me?" How could I have failed to remember him? That workshop had been his introduction, but he had pursued the vision until we were now meeting up at an international clown convention.

10:30 AM: Unpack the experience. It is important for people to talk about this process. Don't ever underestimate what will be going on in people's minds at this point. Though it might sound incredible, some will almost certainly be wondering about some radical change in the whole direction of their life—while others will have found it very hard going, and may be wondering why they ever allowed themselves to get mixed up with such crazy stuff. How you handle the outcome is crucial, so pray and be sensitive to different needs and responses. This doesn't mean you need to have all the answers. Depending on the size of the group and how well they have melded together, choose either to share in twos or small groups, or in the complete group if it's not too big and everyone is happy.

10:45 AM: Coffee. If you've put your back into these exercises, you will need your coffee and something that gives your blood sugar a boost—so maybe also a chocolate biscuit!

11:15 AM: Give a few tips on making up, perhaps by demonstrating on a volunteer. Describe the different types of classic clown: Auguste, white-face or tramp. Ask for examples from popular entertainment that people know. But above all, let people try out the makeup for themselves—there is no substitute for this. As part of your own research for this, it will be worthwhile to scour the local library to see what helpful books they may have. Check out magazines as well, and perhaps have a collage of your findings mounted around the wall. All of this will give helpful inspiration. Once you start to look, you will find clowns everywhere.

If you know a good artist, get him or her to draw some large images for you. In fact, some people in a workshop will find it easier to start by drawing on paper different shapes of eyebrows, mouths and noses before they try it on their own face. It's good to remind people to go back to the clown they saw in their visualization—they may be able to tease more out at this stage.

Encourage people to proceed by trial and error, putting makeup on but not being afraid to wipe it all off again and start over. In practical terms, for the makeup time you need to have tables where tubs of water and pots of paint can stand without fear of spilling. Just in case of any mishaps, protect any special floor covering with plastic. You can get supplies of makeup from your nearest theater shop, and you'll always find that the staff there will happily advise you on the merits of different products. They may seem a bit on the expensive side, but the proper stuff will last you a long time and give very good results. There are basically two kinds—water-based and oil-based—and as a general rule, I have found in Celtic Christian Clowns that the men tend to prefer the oil-based and the women the water-based. But any sort of makeup benefits from using some moisturizer underneath.

Some people have difficulty getting a strong color to go on top of the white. If you're one of them, remove some of the white with a cotton ball to reveal flesh in whatever shape you want, and then paint in the chosen color. Dusting the whole effect with translucent powder will keep the makeup set if you are working for a whole day outside or under theater lighting. It's good to learn how to do this properly in the first instance. Eyelashes will be more noticeable if mascara is used. I remember getting made up in the Usher Hall, a large venue in Edinburgh, only to realize that I had left my mascara at home. Shouting to the other clowns to help, I got no response from the women, but three of the men responded—offering me black, purple or navy! This caused hoots of laughter all round, and helped us relax into the event.

All clown makeup is easily removed using baby oil, baby lotion, or soap and water and cotton wool.

12:30 PM: You definitely deserve a break for lunch now!

1:30 PM: Play with props such as bubbles, juggling balls, spinning plates, musical instruments, and so on—see who can do what. You will have a very unusual group if some of them are not already expert in at least some of these things.

2:00 PM: Get dressed and made-up, before taking the Plunge. Pray together and then go outside in a group, remembering that you need to support one another. Don't have one person abandoning the group to go off and do their own thing. Tread carefully—don't launch into other people's psychological space. You will know where you are welcome. These are the skills we use every day when not in costume. Blow bubbles for a child. Dust the ground with a feather duster for an older person, and step back and laugh. Make a big thing of shaking hands and waving to people across the street. You need to be able to do remarkably few specialized things at this stage. Remember the first game of tag, and move slowly rather than fast. In clowning, as in most other things, you will have fewer disasters if you walk before you try to run. Going out for as little as half an hour to a nearby shopping street or busy place will be quite a sufficient adventure for a first time. If you are going into an actual shopping mall, though, don't forget to get permission first. You might prefer instead to arrange to visit a nursing home or similar venue to brighten someone's day.

3:30 PM: Tea, back at your workshop venue—unless you have been invited to stay and have it in the nursing home. If you have, be warned that one of the first skills you will need to learn is how to take a drink without leaving your makeup in a mess.

4:00 PM: Talk about your experiences, discuss what worked and say if anything was difficult. Try to list what you have learned from this first time outside. You will never again go out so "cold," so it's important to capture all you can from this adventure (without turning it into a painful post-mortem).

4:30 PM: Now is a good time to pursue skills a bit more. Once you have been outside, you'll be able to see the point of them a bit more clearly. Now is the time to introduce juggling, plate spinning, and so on in a serious way. You might already have found earlier that your group has an expert in some or all of these, who can now give a bit of tuition to others. For those who are only capable of flopping in a seat for half an hour, why not show a video on circus skills?

6:00 PM: Take time to worship together. Incorporate what you can from the day: it need not be long, but it should be relevant.

6:30 PM: Dinner: either go home or have a shared meal together. If you have a visiting guest clown, then maybe invite your families and friends to join in and dress for dinner (in clown gear?) and enjoy a contribution from your guest. But don't work him/her to the point of exhaustion.

Sunday

On this day you will need to adjust the timetable to work with your morning service. Whatever time that might be, be sure your clowns meet in good time to makeup before others start to arrive. First-timers might just want to be welcomers, dusting people's shoes as they arrive, or giving out books. If this is your church's first experience of such things, it will likely be a very special occasion for you all. Your visitor may be able to make a contribution to the service, or you may take one of the ideas from elsewhere in this book to include.

Don't be overambitious for this first time. You don't have to play a major role in the service. As a matter of fact, a good way to introduce this kind of thing to the services of a church with no previous experience of it can be for clowns just to welcome worshipers as they arrive, and then to go and sit in the congregation themselves just as they might normally do. Merely being there in clown costume and makeup can give the congregation time to get used to the idea, and to be reassured that this is not a gimmick—though be prepared for the person leading a service to make comments on the appearance of some strange people. A simple clown addition to even a very traditional service could be using the bubbles in prayer, or bringing in the Bible and blowing the dust away (both are described in earlier chapters).

Remember to shake hands with people as they go out, and maybe distribute balloons printed with an appropriate message.

Finally . . . at whatever time you choose to finish, present certificates to those who have lasted the course. This could alternatively be included in the service, or in Saturday night's dinner, but it is a nice way to end. Well, not quite, because for the very end you will want to close with a clown benediction (a benediction blesses people and sends them out after their worship—so in the same way must a clown benediction sum up the events and send people out with hope). Say something like, "Go into all the world as Christ's fools, share the gospel by using the talents God has enriched you with. Turn tears into laughter and so fulfill your calling." Then exchange addresses so people can keep in touch and support one another—and of course plan for stage 2, whatever that might be.

So that's it in a nutshell. I have deliberately kept this outline very basic, so that it will be accessible to most people. I have designed it particularly to help those who have done absolutely nothing in this area at all, as a way of getting started. But I can guarantee that following these simple steps will save you from many of the possible pitfalls—I know that much from experience.

So what are you waiting for? Go for it!

Conclusion

I hope that by now you have caught something of the power of Christian clowning, both in terms of its potential in evangelism and in the development of personal spirituality. It has been a challenging task for me to express in words what is in essence a visual and tactile process. Maybe, in the end, it is a futile undertaking, because—like discipleship itself—clowning is something to be put into practice rather than placed under the microscope.

One of the things I do want to emphasize in rounding this book off is that clowning is not just the latest in a long line of gimmicks that an ailing church can invoke to try to boost its congregations. As I have pointed out in several places, the distinctive ministry of clowns can be traced throughout several periods in the history of the Christian church. Their role has been a bit like that of John the Baptist in the Gospels, who pointed to Jesus and, in effect, said, "Look, here is someone really important—be sure and take notice of what he is saying." Historically, the clown ministers (or Holy Fools as they were known) acted as the divine interrupter. They had the privilege of entering the sanctuary during worship, interrupting the service and, by their "act" or "mime," challenging the participants to take a close look at what they were doing and why. In that connection, they had always operated at the radical edge of corporate spirituality, and it was when they consistently made church leaders into a laughing-stock that they were eventually banished in late medieval times, only to make a reappearance towards the end of the 20th century.

Jesus, of course, frequently found himself in a similar position, challenging the way that mindless tradition could take over even spiritual institutions, as onerous and unnecessary burdens were imposed on worshipers. The Church today, faced with enormous and rapid change in the wider culture, needs to be encouraged to ask some fundamental questions about why we do the things we do, and it seems to me that clowns are uniquely placed to raise such matters. A true Holy Fool will not, however, assume that he or she knows all the answers. Actually, clowns are called on to highlight the important questions and then fade into the background and give space for others to work things out for themselves. This is the exact opposite of the way in which church people sometimes operate, even becoming obsessive about telling people "how it is" and insisting on neat answers when in reality there are none. Most of us know that life simply isn't like this. I discovered this painfully when I lost my daughter. I had more questions than answers. In some ways, I still do, which is why this book has been about affirming that it is all right—spiritually productive, indeed—to have questions. I wonder if the churches in the West have got themselves into such serious decline because we have spent too much time trying to control everything, making sure that people have the same answers as we do, and in the process have forgotten how to be guardians of the right questions.

As I have shared my story, one of the things I have come to appreciate is that people today are searching for safe spaces in which to deal with the experiences that make up their own story of life. By being prepared to be vulnerable, we can allow others the security to examine their own fears. If we Christians present ourselves as people who have it all together (as if we ever could!) we will not be helpful to those who are oppressed. We will only make them feel more like failures. Nor is a false sense of our own inferiority any more helpful: it just suggests that following Jesus is only for losers. But when we tell it the way it is, then others can do the same, a dialogue can happen and a journey can begin.

Understanding the journey that is life is a major concern for growing numbers of people today, who flock to spiritual workshops, seminars and retreats in their thousands. Though this final section of the book is headed "Conclusion," maybe I should have called it "Up to This Point," because for me the story is not yet finished, and the journey may well be about to move off in yet another new direction.

Like most people, faced with the discontinuities of life in a postmodern culture, I regularly find myself asking, "so where do I go from here?" And the more I try to look forward, the more I find myself being called back to where I started. My original entry point into clowning stemmed from my own sense of loss and the consequent need for healing. And that one word—healing—together with the related concept of wholeness is perhaps a good way to sum up what I want to say.

Of course, healing and wholeness can have many different manifestations. I remember the first time I saw the Hollywood movie Patch Adams, in which Robin Williams plays a real-life doctor of that name, and being fascinated by the remarkable outcomes that he has achieved with mentally disturbed patients. Central to his unconventional methodology is clowning. Perhaps I shouldn't have been so surprised, as an American clown named Shobi Dhobi had already been sending me copies of her regular "Hospital Clown Newsletter," and I had myself had at least one interesting experience in relation to clowning and healthcare, when my friend Clownbo went into hospital for surgery and I went to visit him as Valentine. Predictably, perhaps, he didn't notice anything unusual about this (after all, he'd probably seen me in costume at least as much as out of it). But what did surprise me was the enthusiasm with which I was greeted by just about everyone I met, from the person at the door to the doctors and nurses who were moving about the corridors.

While I was with my friend, a constant stream of different members of staff came looking me out, to ask if I would also visit other patients. One doctor in particular brought a woman to see me who had suffered a severe stroke. This woman had not spoken since her illness and had very little means of expressing her needs. I knelt down beside her, held her hands and chatted to her—or maybe babbled would be nearer the truth, because I really didn't have a clue what to say to her. But I could see from her eyes that she was very excited, and she made enormous efforts to squeeze my hand and try to communicate. I was quite delighted, because I could sense that this was a very special moment for her, but I only began to realize the true measure of the response I was evoking when I looked up to the staff who were with her. With a choking voice and glistening eyes, the one pushing the wheelchair said simply, "This is real progress."

Not long after that, I was invited to visit a school for children with special needs. I really had no idea how to approach this either, as the children's levels of disability were so severe that they needed almost one-to-one care constantly. Telling any sort of story would have been a waste of time, for they simply lacked the capacity to engage in that way. So I asked my clown friend Jangle to go along with me, and we just took a huge bag of clown clothes. The children shared lots of laughter as we let them touch and feel all the different fabrics and wigs. I had also made a huge doll out of two stuffed pillows, and we dressed her as a clown, complete with fluorescent wig and bright red shiny shoes. We named her Polly.

Just as the healthcare workers had been, so the teachers in this hard situation were delighted and excited by the stimulus this created for the children, and the ways in which they responded. It was a matter of great excitement for them all when one of the children was featured in a full-color photograph with Valentine on the front page of the local newspaper. Then, on one sunny day something like six months later, I unexpectedly met the same group at an outdoor event attended by many hundreds of children, all of whom struggled with disabilities of some kind. The teachers were ecstatic when they saw the excitement displayed by all the children in one way or another—because they had remembered! This was a real milestone for them.

Not long after that, in the spring of 2000, I visited the city of Baltimore in the USA, where I had been invited to speak at a Holy Week service. The day before the service, my hosts took me past the venue so I could get an idea of the sort of place it was.

One look at the streets around the church confirmed that it was definitely not the sort of place to go to without local knowledge. Guns, drugs, and criminality of all sorts were right there in a very obvious way, and while we were driving by the church the car in which I was travelling was rammed by some youths for no apparent reason. So I was psyched up for something a bit different when I arrived for the service the next night. One thing I did not expect was the numbers that turned up. The church was packed, holding perhaps eight or nine hundred, and it was only later that I discovered there was an overflow crowd of roughly the same size watching through a video link downstairs. The vast majority of them were African Americans, though there was also a visiting choir from Germany—who were not Christians—who had been learning how to sing in traditional African gospel style, and went along because their teacher was one of the organizers of this event. I think it is fair to say that they had never seen anything like it. Nor, in some ways, had I, though I felt really at home with this crowd from the very start. Clowning is of course an interactive medium anyway, and speaking to the kind of audience who not only respond, but make their own contributions all the time, created a very different atmosphere than any Holy Week service I had ever been to in Britain.

The address that night was the Valentine story, for that was what I had been invited to share, and as I told of my own experiences there was a gradually rising crescendo of excitement and enthusiasm throughout the congregation. I concluded by speaking of going out into the street to follow Jesus, and what it might look like through the cross (and it was some street, remember!) As I did so, I walked to the back of the church and towards the door, leaving my husband John to invite those present to have the sign of the cross painted on them so that they too might find the strength and inspiration to engage afresh with the challenges facing them in that community. Though I am always surprised when people respond, I think I knew on that night what would happen next. It seemed as if everyone in that church was up on their feet, and in no time at all the entire place erupted into that kind of holy pandemonium that I had only ever seen on films before. John and I both had huge lines of people wanting us to pray with them and apply the cross to their persons. Fortunately, I had anticipated something like this and went well prepared with large quantities of white paint for dark skins, as well as my regular black paint for the white-face clown.

As we compared notes later, the one thing that had struck us both was the very high proportion of people who shared health needs with us. Whether that was because, in a poor neighborhood, illness was more prevalent, or there was less access to affordable healthcare, I don't know. But healing—in every sense of the word—was what people were seeking. Needless to say, the program that had been planned for the remainder of the evening went out of the window, and it must have been almost midnight by the time we left that place, having prayed with and painted the cross on literally hundreds of people, maybe more.

That, of course, is what it is all about. For me, spiritual clowning is rooted first of all in the Christian doctrines of creation and incarnation—creation, because it affirms that we are all special, made as people in God's image, and therefore to be valued in and of ourselves; and incarnation, because the coming of Christ into our world assures us that this is also God's world, that God is involved with what goes on here, and is to be found even in the darkest of circumstances, whether that be the violence of the streets or the less visible but no less destructive personal struggles of our own souls. Those two angles undoubtedly bring good news into our lives, but without the cross there is no escape, for that is where we discover how to take human suffering seriously. Whatever else may be said about the mystery of pain, the cross bears witness to the fact that Jesus Christ stands alongside us in our hurt. But it also points forward beyond the suffering to an expectation of redemption. The colors of life in my clown paint box constitute a theology of hope and resurrection.

I sometimes feel a bit like Ezekiel, picking his way through fields full of dry bones and seeing God breathe new life into them. When he tried to get to the bottom of the intriguing ministry to which God had called him, he concluded that the only sensible answer to his many questions was, "Only you know that, Lord God" (Ezekiel 37:3). What is Christian clowning all about? Why do such simple stories speak so powerfully? Why have I found healing in such a crazy place, and why have these two simple characters, Valentine and Barni, become a means of wholeness for other people? Although, in the final analysis, God truly is the only one who knows, I have more than a suspicion that it is connected to the fact that clowning both contains and communicates the essence of Christian belief, and in the process embraces all the major doctrines, from creation to future hope. Many things in this postmodern world appear to have no conclusion in the traditional sense of the word, but for a book on clown ministry that is entirely appropriate. For if God really is at the heart of it, who knows what might happen next?

Appendix 1

Creative Bible Study

In chapter 11, I included some stories regarding the use of interactive methods to explore the Bible. What I wrote there will give you the general idea, but here are some more specific instructions and guidelines that you will find helpful.

Bible Stills

This is done in groups of perhaps five or six people, as previously described. I find that people working in groups like this value having specific written instructions to guide them through the process. I would give each member of a group a copy of the following guidelines, on which also I would include the Bible reference for whatever story I may be wanting them to work on. Some stories work better than others, and I have my own favorites, but decide for yourself which ones you will use.

• Imagine you are making a movie, and you are going to present the outline of the story through a series of stills. Read your story carefully, then look at its various sequences and divide it up into different scenes (most of the stories being used easily divide into something like four to six scenes).

• Think about each of the characters in the story (including crowds, if relevant, as well as individuals). What would they be doing in each scene? How would they be sitting, standing, laying down, or whatever? What expressions might they have on their faces? Work out how each member of your group will look in each scene, so as to represent them all.

• Then put your stills together to form a sequence of scenes that will lead through the story. In each sequence you need to be completely motionless, as if you were statues.

• When you present your sequence to the others, they will close their eyes ("curtains down") while you arrange yourselves into the different scenes, and then open their eyes ("curtains up") to look at your stills, so that all they see will be your sequence, not the movement in between.

Bible Rap Stories

I haven't yet included an account of this technique, but it's another one that I have often used. Again, I would divide people into groups (these groups can be slightly bigger if necessary), and give each person a sheet containing the following instructions, which will be self-explanatory if you decide to experiment with this method.

• You are going to present a story by means of phrases that will build on to one another.

• First, read your story carefully, identify its various themes, and think of a phrase (three or four words) that will sum up each theme. Then within the group, decide who will play each theme. The first person starts off, repeating their phrase a couple of times in a rhythmic way. Then the second joins in (the first keeps going), then the third joins them, and so on until you are all saying your phrases at once. If you want to be really adventurous, go for whatever variations on this you feel happy with.

• Now you should think of some actions that you can do, to reflect what you are saying in the words. Put the whole thing together ready to present to the rest of the people who are here.

As with the Bible Stills, some stories work better than others, and you need to give some advance thought to it so that you don't invite people to attempt what is either impossible or could only be done with much practice or prior experience. Here is an example of what the final outcome might be, if your story was the Good Samaritan (Luke 10:29-37).

The traveller (in sporting pose): Run to Jericho—run to Jericho—run to Jericho . . .

The robber (shaking a fist): Beat him/her up—Beat him/her up—Beat him/her up . . .

The priest (nose in air): Worship God—Worship God— Worship God . . .

The Levite (in a hurry): Can't stop now—Can't stop now— Can't stop now . . .

The Samaritan (holding his head in grief): What a mess— what a mess—what a mess . . .

The donkey (bending over to form a back): Take him home— Take him home—Take him home . . .

Innkeeper (rubbing hands in anticipation): Gimme the cash— Gimme the cash—Gimme the cash . . .

Narrator and/or Jesus figure: Who is the real friend—who is the real friend—who is the real friend . . .

Creating a Bible Tableau

I have also described this briefly in chapter 11. Here is a more comprehensive account of what to do. I'll use the story in Luke 5:1-11 as an example, and imagine you are using it in a regular Sunday service.

As a leader, for your preparation you should read the story thoroughly several times, but above all, try to imagine the scene. Don't think just about the visuals, but allow yourself to hear the sounds, sniff the smells, feel the sand, the water, the texture of the rope—and whatever else you discover there. Only your imagination sets the limits. Then in the service, begin to tell the story. Set the scene, using what you have discovered. Tell the story briefly up to the point of Jesus inviting these experienced fishing people to launch out. Don't be afraid to describe the sounds, smells and feelings, as well as the sights. Describe the boat—and then invite people to identify where they feel they might fit into this story. Do they identify with the fishermen, the fish, the mast of the boat, the nets, the water, Jesus, the other boats coming to help, or . . .?

Gradually, build up a picture using the elements that people identify with. Invite people to imagine they really were the things/people they identified with. Some will need to come out to the front to take up a position and follow an action. You can have as many as you like taking part—the more the better, because the real learning takes place as people enter the picture. In a small congregation, build up a simple tableau at the front of the room with as many roles as possible, then include everyone else participating from their seats as waves, other boats, or people watching. In a very large congregation, take care to include everybody. Several groups might do the same thing, or alternatively the people at the extremities of the church could be small boats eagerly coming to help, or small fish, or waves. But be sure to let them all choose individually who or what to be.

Now you are ready for action! Start by doing things in mime: the heave and swell of the sea, the motion of the boat, movements of the fishermen and so on. Encourage people to move as they want—and then to add voices and sounds if they wish. Keep the recreation of the scene going for long enough that a great shoal of fish can be caught, and then for Jesus to give the people in this tableau their new commission: "From now on, you will be catching people," or inviting them to "Come and follow me."

Unpacking the Experience

In all cases of interactive Bible study, it is very important to allow space for people to unpack the experience. Remember, you have invited people to identify themselves with particular characters, and just as participants in more formal role-play exercises need to be given time and space to leave their assumed character, so the same thing applies here. You don't need any specially fancy methodology, but do plan some carefully phrased questions to help people express what they felt while being whoever or whatever they selected, such as:

- Who or what did you choose to be?
- How did it feel to be Peter . . . a net . . . the donkey . . . ?
- What feelings did you have about yourself?
- What feelings did you have about how you related to other people . . . or how they related to you?
- Does the way you felt help you understand anything about the way you feel about Jesus, or your life, or this church, or . . . ?
- Which things were good experiences?
- What were the difficult things?

Remember to allow plenty of time for this—and be prepared for some surprises. The responses will give some key insights into the questions of the participants. People take this much more seriously than you might think, and often come up with quite profound observations and discoveries. As a leader, you need to be prepared to think on your feet as you tie it all together, and respond to what is actually said.

Appendix 2

Some Original Clown Sketches

These are all clown sketches that I have developed and used myself. If you choose to use or adapt them, you need to be sensitive to the needs of your actual audience. Remember what I have said in previous chapters about the dangers of merely replicating what somebody else does. There is no copyright in ideas, and in any case I think of what I have developed as part of God's gift, through me, to the wider community. But if you do use any of them in a context where you have a printed program, it would be nice if you could give me a mention. There is, however, copyright in words, and if you want to reproduce the actual text of any of these sketches you should ask for permission first, by writing to me c/o The Bible Reading Fellowship, First Floor, Elsfield Hall, 15-17 Elsfield Way, Oxford, OX2 8FG.

United Communion

This sketch came out of my involvement with the World Council of Churches, and the need to apply myself to understanding people of different theological and ethnic backgrounds—to hear what they were really saying. This mime sketch gives an opportunity to highlight our denominational idiosyncrasies, the things that we take for granted, but which can so easily take over and have a central place in our Christian worship and witness. The aim of this skit is to recapture the heart of the gospel. It is all done in mime.

Several clowns enter with their differently sized and shaped bags—suitcase, briefcase, Gladstone bag and so on—from which they begin to unpack their portable communion kits. They each represent a different denomination, and the contents of each bag emphasizes the distinctive aspects of the way that particular tradition behaves and believes, especially the way they celebrate communion. Presbyterians have their small cups and neatly sliced squares of bread; Catholics have their wafers and incense; Baptists their grape juice; Episcopalians, Methodists, and others may also be featured, depending on the audience. Each one sets up their own equipment and begins to mime his or her distinctive ritual. Through the door comes a Holy Fool—mirroring Jesus—dressed very simply, and carrying only a rucksack. This clown is surprised and interested as he or she inspects what each of the others is doing. The clown lacks all the necessary credentials to share any of the others' communion services, but still invites the others to join in a circle on the floor, unpacking the rucksack and sharing its simple contents: a loaf of bread and regular bottle of wine.

The sketch may end there, or alternatively the Jesus figure can pack all the fancy equipment belonging to the others into the rucksack, leaving everyone united around the simple symbols he or she has brought.

Praying from the Newspaper

I've already mentioned this sketch in an earlier chapter. Here are some more specific instructions. It requires two or more clowns, together with a specially prepared clown's newspaper—twelve to sixteen sheets of a normal newspaper taped together to make a very large paper when opened, but folded down to normal size to begin with. A park bench is at center stage.

The clowns enter, one carrying the folded newspaper. They sit on the bench and begin reading the paper together, commenting on various news items as they do so, and gradually opening out the newspaper in the process. News items should be decided in advance and should include a variety of subjects, world and national events, but also some directly relevant to the audience—local sports achievements, personal honors, and so on. Each time the paper is unfolded, further news items are identified and commented on, until eventually the clowns will need to stand up on the bench or on chairs to cope with the vast size of the paper. Don't rush this, though: spend plenty of time chatting about the various news items.

When the paper becomes too large to handle, it begins to tear (a skilled clown might somersault through it). At this point the clowns give up, saying that they have had enough news, and in any case they don't know how to handle this ridiculous newspaper. They gather it up, and roll it into a tight ball, and throw it to someone (not a clown) who is prepared to receive it. This might be the minister or another person, who will then hold it aloft in their own hands and, using the various news items already mentioned by the clowns, make it a focus for congregational prayer.

Introducing the Bible Reading

The purpose of this sketch is to draw attention to the Bible and the importance we attach to its message. In the churches of the Reformed tradition, the Bible is often carried in and opened before the minister enters the pulpit, signifying that both congregation and minister are operating under the authority of the Word of God. This has become so commonplace that frequently people miss its intended significance. But when something so familiar is highlighted in a different way, then there can be a reawakening and new appreciation of old truths.

There are various ways to start this sketch. For example, a clown may go before the beadle, or whoever normally carries the Bible, brushing the aisle and making way for the Bible to be brought in—like John the Baptist, the forerunner, inviting people to get ready for Christ's coming. So as to affirm traditional practice, the Bible can still then be taken into the pulpit in the usual way, but instead of being opened immediately, it can be left closed until the clown goes up, opens the Bible and blows on a little fold of paper filled with talcum powder, which has been previously hidden inside it. You can imagine the rest: a cloud of powder will rise up like dust, while the clown simply retreats and sits down. The message conveyed is of blowing the surplus debris or accumulated paraphernalia away and hearing the Word as though for the first time. It may sound amusing, but it is sometimes nearer the truth than we care to admit. I was invited to do this at a large church in Pasadena, California, and decided to use the regular pulpit Bible for the purpose—only to find that it literally fell to pieces in my hands, and needed the addition of absolutely no artificial dust whatever!

Another way of highlighting the Bible's importance can happen at any appropriate time during the service, using a small group of clowns to "interrupt" proceedings. They carry with them a huge box (from a really large appliance, like a freezer or washing machine) decorated like a gift parcel, brightly wrapped and tied. The clowns will find it helpful to chatter to each other through Kazoos. As long as they don't all talk at once, but give one another space as you would in a real conversation, this can sound like effective "clown speak." They make a meal out of carrying the "heavy" box (which is really very light) to the front, accompanied by much huffing and puffing. The person leading the service needs to pause and ask what the fuss is about, and make a comment such as, "Don't you know there's a service going on?"—or whatever. The clowns answer back in Kazoo language, which makes this a very easy dialogue, the initiative coming from the leader and the clowns just responding. The leader might continue with things like, "Oh I see it's a present. Is it for me? But . . . it's not my birthday or my wedding anniversary."

With much miming and exaggerated hand directions, the clowns eventually get the leader to understand that the box must be opened. At the bottom of it all is a book (the smaller the better, relative to the size of the box), and to make it more fun you can include packing such as balloons, maybe with a Christian logo or simple statement on them (for example "God loves you"). The leader makes it clear that he or she was hoping for something more exciting than a book (which of course is a Bible), puts it aside and makes as though to go on with the service. However, the clowns keep on pressing their point (through the Kazoos and with exaggerated gesticulations) until eventually the leader realizes that the book is not just a personal gift to be read for themselves, but is for everyone there. Let the clowns point a passage out in mime, which is then eventually read aloud, at which point the clowns just sit down and listen like everyone else. They have done their job by getting everyone to sit up and take notice, instead of dreaming through the reading.

Fun with a Song

Songs with actions can lend themselves to much play with clowns. Though not my personal favorite, one of the simplest songs that seems to be well known around the world is "Hallelu, Hallelu, Hallelu, Hallelujah, Praise ye the Lord!" Congregations often use it responsively in any case, with one group standing to sing the "Hallelus," and another to sing "Praise ye the Lord." It's easy to make a choir of clowns who can very easily muddle up such simple instructions—bumping into each other, sitting on one another's knees—just try it and you will find lots of things emerge, depending on your clown personalities. Let someone be the choir leader and wave a feather duster for a baton. As well as its effect in a service, you will have enormous fun just getting it ready. You could equally well use another song that you are familiar with.

I remember doing this at an event in Edinburgh, where we gently poked fun at the way some people speak, pronouncing "yes" as "yah." They are not alone in this, of course (at least, not in Britain). So on that occasion there were three groups: the "hallelus," the "praise ye the Lords," and the "yahs." When it came to "Hallelu-yah," the clowns who were the "yahs" raised huge fun hands that someone had made for them, which was also a gentle way of laughing at the charismatic preferences of some in the audience. The fact that they were dressed in tailcoats only added to the humor.

Interpreting a Parable

Sometimes we will use this technique just as a warm-up exercise, only to discover that it can uncover wonderful new ways of telling a Bible story. I remember once using the parable of the Good Samaritan, and the clowns spontaneously acted out the parts, in whatever way they liked. One person read the story, and each time another character or group of characters came into the narrative another clown or clowns joined in. Naturally, we used clown props—like feather dusters instead of stones and hammers such as real robbers might have used. So, for example, instead of beating the traveller up, they tickled him to distraction with the dusters. Then two other clowns became the donkey, and so on.

It's surprising how much fun you can have trying out something like this. Even if you don't use all the material outside the clown group, you may find some ideas that you can use on another occasion. It's a very good technique for loosening up before you work.

The Heart Sketch

There are many variations of this sketch. I start as if I was doing a keep-fit or aerobics routine, and play with standard clown gags in the process: for example, when I can't touch my toes, I bend my knee and lift my foot up to my hand. If I do this with another clown, they will be eating healthy food like a stick of celery while my prop will be something like a lollipop. That way we can make much play of me eating the lollipop behind the other's back, until eventually I am caught out and made to do the exercises. I also use an exaggerated tape measure for my partner to measure me with. As part of the routine, I usually include something quite strenuous, or jog round the church so I can plausibly pretend I am out of breath. I then make a big thing of finding my pulse, and when I can't find it in my wrist or neck then I become alarmed and test out the pulses of others who are watching. This can be great fun.

Eventually, I find my heartbeat, reach into my jacket, take my heart out of my chest and start to play with it. I throw it up and catch it. I throw it to others and get them to throw it back. People really do need to use their imagination, and invariably love joining in. When they do this, you know that they have cottoned on! I eventually become blasé and start to throw it really high, just managing to catch it a couple of times before I miss it and it shatters on the ground. Obviously devastated, I try to pick the bits up (here some technical mime skills using "clicks," for example, will give a professional look—to do this pick up an imaginary fragile piece of heart between the thumb and forefinger, pause, flick the wrist slightly and freeze before continuing —the flicking action is known as a "click"), but the pieces just won't fit together.

I then hear a voice from above, which turns out to be The Voice and (all still in mime: no words) God invites me to hand my heart over. I do this with the greatest of reluctance, and have a great show of tears. But then a moment later The Voice comes again, and I receive my heart back completely intact. My appreciation is obvious (and exaggerated), and I make it look as if I'm going to play with it again—but decide it's better to tuck it safely back where it belongs. As I leave, I will pause to blow a kiss in thanks to God.

Once, when I was practicing this with another clown in her kitchen before going to an event, we were struggling to make our hands work to imitate a beating heart. You can do this by putting thumbs and fingers of both hands together—you will see that this can make a heart shape with your thumbs at the top, and with a little jerking movement it will look like a heart beating. You have to believe it yourself before you can convince others.

My friend's sister-in-law was there, and though she didn't really approve of all this clowning stuff she was still happy to look after my friend's kids while we were at the event. But she is a medic, and for that reason she just couldn't help being drawn into our discussion, advising us on how to mime a living heart in such a way that it would look authentic. We were doing just a single beat, but she reminded us that the real thing has a double beat. Only a doctor would have known the difference, but her advice certainly enhanced the performance.

Balloon Modeling

This has become very popular quite apart from clowning, and balloons and books about modeling are readily available. With just a few balloon models you can easily tell a story—all it takes is a bit of practice.

Bubbles

These are a great way to get something going, especially if you don't feel competent in some of the more energetic or acrobatic things I've talked about. Literally anyone can blow bubbles. You can get all sorts of devices from the simple tub in your local paper shop to contraptions that make bubbles as long as thirty feet. The big ones are nothing like as hard as they can look, and they work especially well for outdoor events, though the humidity of the air makes a big difference to how well they work. The best way to start experimenting with this is to buy a complete kit of bubble maker with instructions, which you can get in most toy shops or bookstores. A widely available one (which also works very effectively) comes packaged with a book by John Cassidy, called *The Unbelievable Bubble Book* (Klutz Press, 1987). Smaller ones work well for use in responsive prayers, as I've explained in a previous chapter. Just blow the bubbles, say a simple prayer, and use a response such as "As the bubbles burst (or soar—it depends on the humidity) we know God will hear our prayers." Try different responses, but always keep them simple.

Handshaking

It will surprise you how welcoming people into church or greeting them in the street will become a sketch in itself. You may choose to be a silent clown, though even in that guise you will discover how to carry on a whole dialogue without saying a word. Saying farewell also brings its own rewards, as people chat. I love to do "high fives" with kids who line up expecting the usual handshake—their eyes light up because suddenly life as they normally experience it has burst through conventional ecclesiology.

Appendix 3

Destination Bethlehem

Although the main focus of my ministry has been on clowning, the title of this book—*Clowns, Storytellers, Disciples*—has given me the opportunity to share some other examples of the use of the arts in Christian ministry. In this appendix, I want to recount how a particular story that came to be known as "Destination Bethlehem" was told to a specific community.

As I said in chapter 11, I got my inspiration for this from a small church at Newton Junction in New Hampshire, and their annual outdoor Christmas tableau. But the opportunity to do something about it came in the first week of January 1998, while I was living in Stirling. I had a call from my friend and minister at the time, Alasdair Black. Would I consider working on something for young families the following December? I was surprised to receive this invitation just the week after the Christmas holidays ended, but an unsatisfactory experience of so-called "creative worship" a couple of weeks before had left him convinced that he did not want a repeat in a year's time.

I took quite a long time to consider my response, because I knew that I did not want to do "something" unless I could do it well and imaginatively. In fact, it was not until that summer, while I was in-line skating by the beach at Santa Barbara in California, that I finally knew the way forward. I decided that I wanted to tell the Christmas story in an accessible way to the young families in our town. I remembered how excited my own children had been when each of them heard this story for the first time, and I was eager to repeat that sense of joyous discovery for the families in our community, for whom the only accessible version of the Christmas story was about spending money and having parties. If I could persuade the church to do that, then I would say "yes" to the invitation.

On my return to Scotland, I took a walk through the center of the town, past the church. As I looked across the busy street from the other side of the road, I began to see the building in a new way. Instead of thinking about what I knew was inside, I looked at the church as the pedestrians saw it: a substantial stone wall as high as the shops next door, with a small arch leading through to the church, which was built behind and towered above it.

It occurred to me that the one thing today's families like to do is to go to places where they are actually able to enter into the experience of the story, whether it's a museum, a wildlife center, or whatever. As it happened, this church building—though old— had been totally refurbished and imaginatively divided and extended in such a way that there were endless passageways and spaces that could easily form the basis of a trip back in time to the world of the Bible. It was obvious from the outset that this was not an enterprise that any one individual could carry through unaided, and as a way of testing out the possibilities, I floated my ideas informally with one of the leaders in the church. He was immediately very keen, and in due course became my best ally and facilitator. The fact that he was also a professional architect came in very useful when we began to turn the church into ancient Bethlehem. Not only did he work out how the building could be made to achieve our objectives, but he also led the way in creating confidence in the project among people who may have been inclined to look on it as yet another of my weird ideas. They knew that an architect could be trusted to look after the building, so I took this as a good sign and agreed "to have a go."

My first step was to ask for a five-minute slot in the morning services to "share the vision" with people. I invited anyone who was interested to meet the next week. I was surprised at how many people came along—and at who they were, for they were mostly people who did not usually take leading roles in church life, but who obviously saw a potential for using their diverse skills in this rather different Christmas event.

What I wanted to do was to use our building to give people a feel of the journey to Bethlehem that was undertaken by Mary and Joseph that first Christmas. So, after not more than about three months of planning, we found ourselves, on the Sunday before Christmas, about to embark on the journey of a lifetime. In late afternoon, just as the shopping center across the road from the church was about to close, a guard of Roman soldiers marched along the street to announce where people could join the queue to go to Bethlehem. Actually, people had already begun lining up outside the church long before this. As they came in through the arched wall, they crept past a stable, complete with live donkey, between serious-looking Roman soldiers. I don't know if I had ever previously imagined that the men in our church would get dressed up like this, but they all seemed to enjoy it. Once inside, visitors joined the queue at border control to be given a passport and have their papers stamped. They had to collect a certain number of stamps in order to get past the bureaucrats, who likewise were dressed in period costume. A good number of these were members of a regular church group for people with various learning disabilities, along with other members of the congregation, of all ages. The section of the church they were standing in had been transformed from its regular use as a coffee lounge and library to become a village street in an ancient Middle Eastern town, all of it designed by a primary school teacher, with assistance from our architect and a team of willing helpers.

For logistical reasons, it was necessary for the next stage of the journey to pass through what was normally a lecture theater. This was quite a difficult transition, which gave birth to another bright idea from the design team. A dark tunnel was created with black cloths covered in stars and pinpricks of light, so that the furnishings of the lecture theater were not visible. The tunnel had quite a spooky feel, which allowed many children who like to be "just a little bit scared" to experience as much fear as they needed. When they emerged at the other end, they found themselves in an oriental marketplace—actually a sports hall—totally and realistically transformed by stalls, straw, authentically low levels of lighting, people in costume, and live hens and ducks scurrying under foot. At the stalls, we were all able to collect everything needed for a long and arduous journey in time, from candles to water. It was even possible to stock up on food, freshly cooked on a stove and providing a real taste of the East, all wrapped up in authentic vine leaves. Every so often, a Roman soldier who was standing warming himself by the fire, barked instructions to the "peasants." I actually saw one normally mischievous nine-year-old boy flinch and move nearer to his mother, not realizing that the soldier was someone who was actually a good family friend.

From the marketplace, which was in the basement of the building, people then wound their way up the stairs, past the sheep (yes, real ones) in a pen, before eventually arriving in the sanctuary. With the help of many bales of straw donated (like the animals) by a local farmer, the front of the church had become a stable, while the space above our heads and up into the vaulted ceiling was festooned with stars to look like the Milky Way. At the back of the church, our clever teacher had produced an outline of the town of Bethlehem in silhouette with tiny Christmas lights blinking at every window. People streamed in, until they had to start squeezing in, and one church leader said to me in a panicked voice, "I don't think we can let any more people in. Who are these people anyway? I don't know most of them." A major problem for some, but that one comment fairly lifted my spirits.

The two anchorpeople were the innkeeper and the innkeeper's wife, who introduced the refrain and actions to one of Steve Fischbacher's songs (he's mentioned in chapter 4). The song in question was "Angry Hotel Man," which comes from Steve's CD *Just Imagine.* During the run-up to this event, I had come across an ecumenical children's choir who performed this music and some other songs, including several composed by their leader, while we built up a tableau of the Christmas story. The idea was that the audience would be able to join in the refrain of "Angry Hotel Man" from time to time.

When it was apparent that most people had squeezed in (probably something like 800 of them, a significant percentage of the population of a small town like Stirling), the Roman guard from outside marched through the church in silence, twice round the perimeter and back out again, the lights were dimmed, and the flustered innkeeper and his wife came bustling in from different directions at the back of the church, looking for more bedding and causing a general stir in the process. The audience absolutely loved it. Andy and Claire, who played the innkeeper and wife, had a rough draft of what they would say, and had practiced together, but the entire thing was made easier for all concerned by not having to rehearse a tight script. Weary families came to the innkeeper only to be sent away—first one, then another. When the innkeeper's wife heard him send the third couple away, and saw the pregnant wife, she berated her husband until he eventually solved the problem by offering them the stable for the night.

At this point, the focus moved to the back of the church (which was in darkness, the various episodes of the story being picked out by spotlights). Here, a very bright star appeared, being carried high by Alison, dressed as an angel with a retinue of toddling angels in her wake (mostly little girls and some boys who were members of our church families). They paused to look up at the back of the church, where a bunch of rough-looking shepherds were standing, while the choir sang a song about the shepherds. The angels with the star continued on their way to the stable, where by this point a new baby had arrived to join Mary and Joseph, and so of course the innkeeper was woken again. The shepherds were beckoned to come and see, which they did in a rowdy and raucous fashion, trying to outrun each other. These shepherds were an interesting group of teenage boys who met in the church on a midweek evening under the leadership of

Christians who were trying to reach out to city-center kids who often found themselves on the wrong side of the law. If they had been asked to be in a play, they certainly would not have agreed, but being asked to create a general commotion as shepherds really appealed to them and let them integrate in a way that surprised themselves as well as the church people.

At the stable, the rowdy shepherds fell silent, mingling with the angels and the travellers, while the sound of a baby gurgling could be heard on tape (although "Mary" was a young mother and "Jesus" was her own baby, we couldn't be sure in advance that he would gurgle or cry on cue). The innkeeper was desperate for some sleep by this stage, and the story continued something like this.

Innkeeper: Angels, shepherds, travellers, will I ever get any sleep?

Wife: Oh hush! You'll waken the baby.

Innkeeper: I'll waken the baby!

He settles down to try to get some sleep—she keeps looking out—spots kings coming—rushes to change and fuss about her hair.

The choir sings about the kings.

Wife wakens innkeeper and the resplendent kings move sedately down the aisle to present their gifts to the baby.

Everyone joins in the chorus from "Angry Hotel Man," which they now know well, having joined in it several times already, while the innkeeper and his wife go and invite other hotel guests (members of the audience) to come and see the baby.

At this point, everything became very hushed by the use of dimmed lighting and soft music. Mary stood center-stage, and while she held her baby high the choir sang a song about Emmanuel, the coming of God into our world. You could have heard the proverbial pin drop. Then everyone joined in singing "Away in a Manger," and along the rows people were encouraged to pass the light from one candle to another till the place was ablaze with light. The angels and other children danced with streamers, and others joined in—this celebration being interrupted only by the innkeeper's wife exclaiming, "This baby's never going to get any sleep—come down to the kitchen and have a nice cup of tea—I'll put the kettle on."

The innkeeper, who had by now forgotten he was tired, invited the entire audience to join in the party, and Christmas music continued while everyone was ushered downstairs to the kitchen where there was indeed a feast waiting for us all to enjoy.

We had invited the people of our community to enter into the Christmas story with us, and they responded with enthusiasm. We were not trying to rewrite the story. Rather, the starting point was looking at our resources and asking what might be possible. That included the building, the available people, and our wider community. We then determined how best to retell the story that we all knew so well.

I took on the job of liaising with the arts department in the local council to ensure that Destination Bethlehem, as it was known, would be listed in the official council program for that Christmas season. Kate was one of the young mothers in the church, whose experience in editorial work enabled us to have good publicity and press releases. I also coordinated the entire event with the help of Jenny, another schoolteacher. The project was made possible for an ordinary church by breaking everything down into manageable-sized pieces. After all, the months up to Christmas are pressurized enough for everyone, without the church adding to that burden. What we were aiming for was a process that would allow those participating to be able to reflect more meaningfully on the incarnation as a result of being part of this venture, in addition to telling the story to our community. One person designed the soldiers' costumes and found willing participants. Another invited her farming friends to provide the animals and helped with decorating the building. Brian, the architect, coordinated everything to do with the building, including health and safety concerns. Someone else supervised the angels, another encouraged the shepherds. A different couple organized the marketplace, while yet others worked on passport control.

People were not coerced into roles they felt uncomfortable with: mostly they offered to participate, and took on jobs they knew they were good at. This meant we had no square pegs in round holes, which in turn led to more fulfillment for those involved, and less angst for the organizers. If any one job looked as if it could get out of hand, we just broke it down into smaller, more manageable pieces. In the process, other people offered Christmas lights, props and materials of all kinds, and were eager to get involved in whatever ways they could. We had offers of sound and lighting equipment. In fact, the entire vision generated so much spontaneous enthusiasm that it would be impossible to list everyone who contributed in some way.

The biggest nightmare was getting everyone together for a rehearsal. It would have been dull, boring and too demanding to have everyone there all the time. So we operated on the assumption that everyone would take responsibility for sorting out their own little bit of the program, and somehow, amazingly, it came together on the night.

You could do this in your community. I don't mean by copying our venture—but you could think through your own resources and dream the possibilities. Always begin with your resources and your venue, and a very large dose of imagination. Think on the grand scale, and work with the outstanding visions to begin with. Of course, there will have to be compromises in due course, but don't start with them. Virtually none of those who were involved in this event would have described themselves as actors. But by working with the skills that people had, we were able to produce something that had a significant impact not only in the life of the church, but also of the wider community.

Other Books
on the Arts in Ministry

General

Adams, Doug, and Diane Apostolos-Cappadona. *Art as Religious Studies.* New York: Crossroad, 1987.

Adams, Doug, and Diane Apostolos-Cappadona. *Art, Creativity & the Sacred.* New York: Crossroad, 1984.

Beall, Patricia. *The Folk Arts in God's Family.* London: Hodder & Stoughton, 1984.

Begbie, Jeremy S. *Voicing Creation's Praise.* Edinburgh: T&T Clark, 1991.

Drane, John. *The McDonaldization of the Church: Spirituality, Creativity, and the Future of the Church.* London: Darton Longman & Todd, 2000.

Fischer, Kathleen R. *The Inner Rainbow.* Mahwah, N.J.: Paulist Press, 1983.

von Oech, Roger. *A Whack on the Side of the Head.* New York: Warner Books, 1990.

Webber, Robert E., ed. *Music and the Arts in Christian Worship.* The Complete Library of Christian Worship 4/2. Nashville: Star Song, 1994.

Wink, Walter. *Transforming Bible Study.* 2nd ed. Nashville: Abingdon Press, 1990.

Clowning and Mime

Adams, Douglas. *The Prostitute in the Family Tree.* Louisville: Westminster John Knox Press, 1997.

Bain, Roly. *Fools Rush In.* New York: HarperCollins, 1993.

Forbes, Patrick. *The Gospel of Folly.* East Wittering, United Kingdom: Angel Press, 1988.

Frost, Michael. *Jesus the Fool.* Sydney: Albatross, 1994.

Hyers, Conrad. *And God Created Laughter.* Louisville: John Knox Press, 1987.

Liebenow, Mark. *Is there Fun after Paul?* San Jose, Calif.: Resource Publications, 1987.

Litherland, Janet. *The Clown Ministry Handbook.* 4th ed. Colorado Springs: Meriwether, 1990.

Litherland, Janet. *Everything New and Who's Who in Clown Ministry.* Colorado Springs: Meriwether, 1993.

Noble, Philip D. *Fool of the Kingdom.* Colorado Springs: Meriwether, 1996.

Shaffer, Floyd. *Clown Ministry.* Loveland, Colo.: Group Books, 1984.

Stevenson, Geoffrey, and Judith Stevenson. *Steps of Faith: A Practical Introduction to Mime and Dance.* Eastbourne, United Kingdom: Kingsway, 1984.

Stewart, Elizabeth-Anne. *Jesus the Holy Fool.* Lanham, Md.: Sheed & Ward, 1999.

Whedbee, J. William. *The Bible and the Comic Vision.* Cambridge: Cambridge University Press, 1998.

Dance

Adams, Doug, and Diane Apostolos-Cappadona, eds. *Dance As Religious Studies.* New York: Crossroad, 1990.

Adams, Doug. *Dancing Christmas Carols.* San Jose, Calif.: Resource Publications, 1978.

De Sola, Carla. *The Spirit Moves: Handbook of Dance & Prayer.* Sharing Company, 1977.

Fisher, Constance. *Dancing with Early Christians.* Sharing Company, 1983.

Fisher, Constance. *Dancing Festivals of the Church Year.* Sharing Company, 1986.

Gagne, Ronald, Thomas Kane, and Robert VerEecke. *Introducing Dance in Christian Worship.* Portland, Ore.: Pastoral Press, 1984.

Jones, Mary. *God's People on the Move.* Drummoyne, Aus.: Christian Dance Fellowship of Australia, 1988.

Stevenson, Geoffrey and Judith Stevenson. *Steps of Faith: A Practical Introduction to Mime and Dance.* Eastbourne, United Kingdom: Kingsway, 1984.

Storytelling

Bausch, William J. *Storytelling, Imagination and Faith.* Mystic, Conn.: 23rd Publications, 1984.

Boomershine, Thomas E. *Story Journey: An Invitation to the Gospel as Storytelling.* Nashville: Abingdon Press, 1988.

Furnish, Dorothy Jean. *Experiencing the Bible with Children.* Nashville: Abingdon Press, 1990.

Moynahan, Michael E. *Once Upon a Parable.* Mahwah, N.J.: Paulist Press, 1984.

Tilley, Terrence W. *Story Theology.* Collegeville, Minn.: Liturgical Press, 1990.

Note: most of these books are in print and should be easily available. The others will be found in any good library.

Notes

1. For an accessible introduction to this approach, see James S. Woodward and Stephen Pattison, eds., *The Blackwell Reader in Pastoral and Practical Theology* (Oxford: Blackwell, 2000).
2. John Drane, *The McDonaldization of the Church* (London: Darton Longman & Todd, 2000).
3. Subsequently published as Raymond Fung, *The Isaiah Vision* (Geneva: World Council of Churches, 1992).
4. For John's reflections on this experience, see his book *Cultural Change and Biblical Faith* (Milton Keynes, United Kingdom: Paternoster Press, 2000), 128-153.
5. Robert Boyd Munger, *My Heart—Christ's Home,* illustrated edition (Downer's Grove, Ill.: InterVarsity Press, 1992; originally 1954).
6. Philip's own story is told in Philip D. Noble, *Fool of the Kingdom* (Colorado Springs: Meriwether Publishing, 1996).
7. The video version is produced by Evangelical Films, Danbury Common Old Mission, The Common, Danbury, Chelmsford, Essex CM3 4EE.
8. Janet Litherland, *The Clown Ministry Handbook,* 4th ed. (Colorado Springs: Meriwether Publishing, 1990); quotations are from page 3.
9. Floyd Shaffer, *Clown Ministry* (Loveland, Colo.: Group Books, 1984), 6.
10. Walter Wangerin Jr., *Ragman and Other Cries of Faith* (San Francisco: HarperSanFrancisco, 1984).
11. In *Common Ground* (Edinburgh: St Andrew Press, 1998), 13.
12. Don S. Browning, *A Fundamental Practical Theology* (Minneapolis: Fortress Press, 1991), 8.
13. See John Drane and Olive M. Fleming Drane, *Family Fortunes: Faith-full Caring for Today's Families,* 2nd ed. (London: Darton Longman & Todd, 2004).
14. British Council of Churches Consultative Group on Ministry among Children, *The Child in the Church* (London: British Council of Churches, 1984), 24. See also Jeff Astley, "Tradition and Experience: conservative and liberal models for Christian education," in Jeff Astley and David Day (eds), *The Contours of Christian Education* (Great Wakering, United Kingdom: McCrimmon, 1992), 41-53.
15. Albert Mehrabian, *Silent Messages* (New York: Penguin, 1971).
16. More specific instructions on how to do this sketch are in appendix 2 at the back of the book.
17. Michael Perry (ed), *The Dramatized Bible* (London: Marshall Pickering, 1989).